Angular 2 Components

A quick and concise guide to Angular 2 Components

Nir Kaufman

Thierry Templier

Pack<t>

BIRMINGHAM - MUMBAI

Angular 2 Components

First published: November 2016

Production reference: 1211116

Published by Packt Publishing Ltd.
Livery Place
35 Livery Street
Birmingham B3 2PB, UK.

ISBN 978-1-78588-234-0

www.packtpub.com

Credits

Authors
Nir Kaufman
Thierry Templier

Reviewers
Robin Böhm
Daniel Zen

Commissioning Editor
Sarah Crofton

Acquisition Editor
Meeta Rajani

Technical Editor
Narsimha Pai

Copy Editor
Laxmi Subramanian

Proofreader
Safis Editing

Indexers
Hemangini Bari
Pratik Shirodkar

Production Coordinators
Deepika Naik
Shantanu N. Zagade

Cover Work
Deepika Naik

About the Authors

Nir Kaufman is the Head of Angular Development at 500Tech, a leading front-end consultancy in Israel. He is a passionate JavaScript developer, an international speaker, and an Angular evangelist.

Nir runs three local Angular community meetup groups in Israel. He also collaborates with other local Angular communities around the world.

Thierry Templier is a senior full stack developer with 17 years of experience. He has been a JavaScript addict for a long time now and started to work with the early versions of the language. He has a particular passion for Angular 2 and loves to help developers to use this framework, particularly on the StackOverflow website, where he has answered more than 1,900 questions.

He also enjoys writing articles to promote and explain Angular 2's specific features on his blog (`https://medium.com/@ttemplier/`) and on the Restlet blog (`http://restlet.com/blog/author/thierry-templier/`).

Thanks to Nir, Meeta, and Narsimha for taking me on board and working with me on this project. Thanks to my beloved wife and son, Séverine and Maël, for their daily support.

About the Reviewers

Robin Böhm is a Germany based passionate trainer for Angular. He is also the co-founder of the AngularJS.DE platform, which is the biggest community for Angular in Germany. Together with his team, he offers intensive workshops and trainings for web development with Angular. Since 2013, they have successfully trained over 5000 developers from freelance developers to employees of large German corporate (DAX) companies.

Daniel Zen is a MIT graduate in Computer Science Engineering and has been teaching and writing software for the past three decades. He has taught computer programming and Agile methodologies at NYU, The New School, and at numerous Fortune 500 companies. He has worked on large-scale art projects, as well as interactive installations at the Museum of Science in Boston and The Milk Gallery in NYC. A former consultant to both Google and Pivotal Labs, Zen is now focused on zen.digital, a full stack JavaScript training and consulting company.

www.PacktPub.com

eBooks, discount offers, and more

Did you know that Packt offers eBook versions of every book published, with PDF and ePub files available? You can upgrade to the eBook version at www.PacktPub.com and as a print book customer, you are entitled to a discount on the eBook copy. Get in touch with us at customercare@packtpub.com for more details.

At www.PacktPub.com, you can also read a collection of free technical articles, sign up for a range of free newsletters and receive exclusive discounts and offers on Packt books and eBooks.

Mapt

https://www.packtpub.com/mapt

Get the most in-demand software skills with Mapt. Mapt gives you full access to all Packt books and video courses, as well as industry-leading tools to help you plan your personal development and advance your career.

Why subscribe?

- Fully searchable across every book published by Packt
- Copy and paste, print, and bookmark content
- On demand and accessible via a web browser

Table of Contents

Preface

Angular 2 is a leap forward from the previous Angular 1.x framework, which became the most popular frontend JavaScript framework in history.

It is a complete re-write, an up-to-date platform that is built upon web standards and modern APIs. With Angular 2, you can build JavaScript applications aimed at the browser, server, mobile, and desktop, thanks to an architecture that decoupled the view layer of Angular from the platform core and services.

This book will be focused on the UI layer of Angular: components. We will explore the rich API and multiple options available for building and composing UI components for powerful user interfaces and views.

What this book covers

Chapter 1, Angular 2 Component Architecture, provides an overview of the existing popular architectural patterns for building frontend applications, and the new approach that relys on composing self-contained custom components.

Chapter 2, Setting Up an Angular 2 Development Environment with angular-cli, covers setting up the development environment with angular-cli.

Chapter 3, The TypeScript Primer, covers the basics of the TypeScript language and what you need to know about TypeScript.

Chapter 4, Building a Basic Component, covers the steps to build a basic component.

Chapter 5, Building Dynamic Components, covers the steps to transform your static component into a dynamic component using core directives and data binding.

Chapter 6, Component Communication, covers different ways to make your components communicate with each other.

Chapter 7, Putting It All Together, covers building the accordion component and the component life cycle.

Chapter 8, Integrating Third-Party Components, covers the integration of a tooltip widget from the popular Bootstrap library.

Chapter 9, Angular 2 Directives, covers the usage of directives in Angular 2.

What you need for this book

You need to know how to read and write JavaScript. Other technologies, such as C# or Java, may help you understand the syntax, but are not mandatory.

Some experience with web development and related technologies such as HTML and CSS is required, so make sure you are familiar with that.

Who this book is for

If you are a frontend developer with some experience in Angular who wants to understand Angular 2 components and use them to create powerful user interfaces, then this book is for you.

This books is also for angular 1.x developers who want to upgrade their knowledge and skills.

Conventions

In this book, you will find a number of text styles that distinguish between different kinds of information. Here are some examples of these styles and an explanation of their meaning.

Code words in text, database table names, folder names, filenames, file extensions, pathnames, dummy URLs, user input, and Twitter handles are shown as follows: "We can include other contexts through the use of the `include` directive."

A block of code is set as follows:

```
class Product {
  private id: number;
  private color: string;

  constructor(id:number, color:string) {
    this.id = id;
    this.color = color;
  }
}
```

Any command-line input or output is written as follows:

```
$ npm uninstall -g angular-cli
$ npm cache clean
```

New terms and **important words** are shown in bold. Words that you see on the screen, for example, in menus or dialog boxes, appear in the text like this: "Clicking the **Next** button moves you to the next screen."

> Warnings or important notes appear in a box like this.

> Tips and tricks appear like this.

Reader feedback

Feedback from our readers is always welcome. Let us know what you think about this book—what you liked or disliked. Reader feedback is important for us as it helps us develop titles that you will really get the most out of.

To send us general feedback, simply e-mail feedback@packtpub.com, and mention the book's title in the subject of your message.

If there is a topic that you have expertise in and you are interested in either writing or contributing to a book, see our author guide at www.packtpub.com/authors.

Customer support

Now that you are the proud owner of a Packt book, we have a number of things to help you to get the most from your purchase.

Downloading the example code

You can download the example code files for this book from your account at http://www.packtpub.com. If you purchased this book elsewhere, you can visit http://www.packtpub.com/support and register to have the files e-mailed directly to you.

You can download the code files by following these steps:

1. Log in or register to our website using your e-mail address and password.
2. Hover the mouse pointer on the **SUPPORT** tab at the top.
3. Click on **Code Downloads & Errata**.
4. Enter the name of the book in the **Search** box.
5. Select the book for which you're looking to download the code files.
6. Choose from the drop-down menu where you purchased this book from.
7. Click on **Code Download**.

You can also download the code files by clicking on the **Code Files** button on the book's webpage at the Packt Publishing website. This page can be accessed by entering the book's name in the **Search** box. Please note that you need to be logged in to your Packt account.

Once the file is downloaded, please make sure that you unzip or extract the folder using the latest version of:

* WinRAR / 7-Zip for Windows
* Zipeg / iZip / UnRarX for Mac
* 7-Zip / PeaZip for Linux

The code bundle for the book is also hosted on GitHub at `https://github.com/PacktPublishing/Angular-2-Components`. We also have other code bundles from our rich catalog of books and videos available at `https://github.com/PacktPublishing/`. Check them out!

Downloading the color images of this book

We also provide you with a PDF filethathascolorimagesofthescreenshots/diagrams used in this book. The color images will help you better understand the changes in the output. You can download this filefrom `https://www.packtpub.com/sites/default/files/downloads/Angular2Components_ColorImages.pdf`.

Errata

Although we have taken every care to ensure the accuracy of our content, mistakes do happen. If you find a mistake in one of our books—maybe a mistake in the text or the code—we would be grateful if you could report this to us. By doing so, you can save other readers from frustration and help us improve subsequent versions of this book. If you find any errata, please report them by visiting http://www.packtpub.com/submit-errata, selecting your book, clicking on the **Errata Submission Form** link, and entering the details of your errata. Once your errata are verified, your submission will be accepted and the errata will be uploaded to our website or added to any list of existing errata under the Errata section of that title.

To view the previously submitted errata, go to https://www.packtpub.com/books/content/support and enter the name of the book in the search field. The required information will appear under the **Errata** section.

Piracy

Piracy of copyrighted material on the Internet is an ongoing problem across all media. At Packt, we take the protection of our copyright and licenses very seriously. If you come across any illegal copies of our works in any form on the Internet, please provide us with the location address or website name immediately so that we can pursue a remedy.

Please contact us at copyright@packtpub.com with a link to the suspected pirated material.

We appreciate your help in protecting our authors and our ability to bring you valuable content.

Questions

If you have a problem with any aspect of this book, you can contact us at questions@packtpub.com, and we will do our best to address the problem.

1
Angular 2 Component Architecture

The way we think about web applications has changed. The goal of this chapter is to provide an overview of the existing popular architectural patterns for building frontend applications, and the new approach that relies on composing self-contained custom components.

Understanding the architectural pattern that was implemented in Angular 1 will help you migrate your existing application to Angular 2 in the future. In this chapter, we will discuss those topics:

- Overview of the Model-View-Controller pattern
- Angular 1 implementation of model, view, and ViewModel
- Moving from MVVM to components
- An example of the Angular 2 components architecture

The Model-View-Controller pattern

This is an architectural design pattern for implementing user interfaces, which has been used for many years for desktop GUI.

It divides the application into three distinct parts:

- **Model**: This is responsible for storing the actual data
- **View**: This is the presentation layer that renders the data to the user
- **Controller**: The glue between the model and the view

The following diagram describes the relationships between those parts:

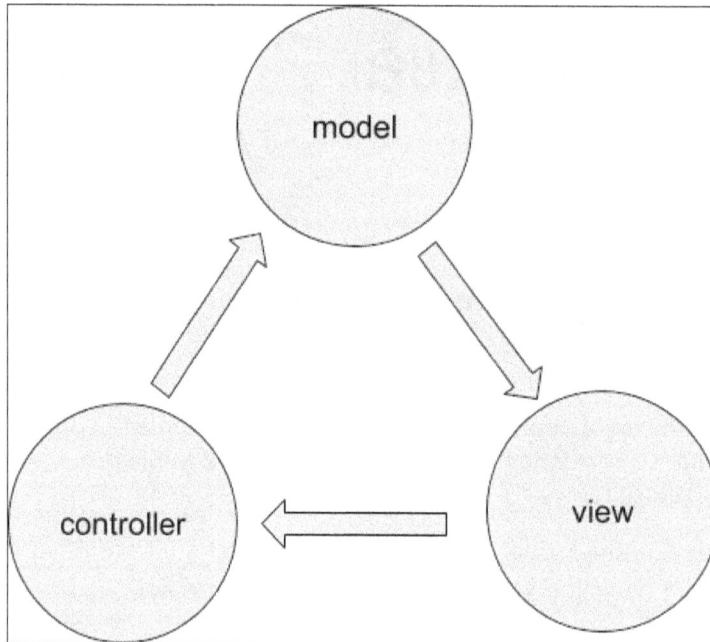

This pattern describes the communication between those parts. The **view** reflects the data in the model, but cannot alter the data directly in the model. It is common to describe the relationship between the model and the view as read only (the view can only read from the model). The view uses the **controller** by invoking methods and changing attributes. The **controller** updates the model, which causes the view to update and render the new data.

MVC, which was originally developed for desktop applications, has been widely adopted as an architecture for building single page web applications and can be found in all the popular client-side frameworks, including Angular.

MVC in Angular 1

Angular 1 implements a variation of the classic MVC, which is known by the name **Model View ViewModel** (**MVVM**). This pattern describes different roles and communication between the parts:

- **Model**: This holds the data or acts as data access layer
- **View**: Like MVC, this is the presentation layer
- **ViewModel**: This is an abstraction of the view that is bound to the view

The following diagram describes the relationships between those parts with the terminology of Angular 1:

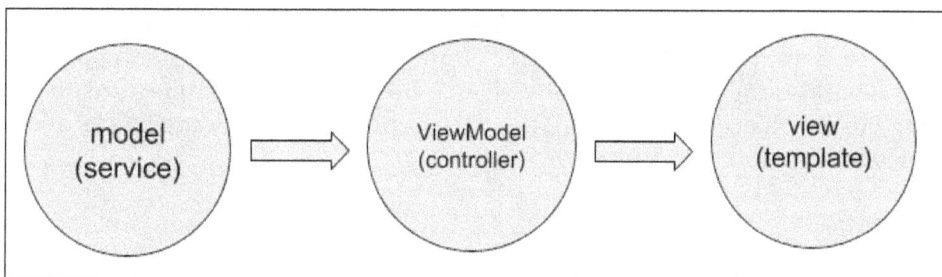

The **ViewModel** in Angular 1 is an object named: '$scope' that is constructed by an Angular controller. We do not always interact with this object directly. It's binding to the view is two-way (In Angular, we refer to the view as a 'Template'). The ViewModel can read and alter the data on the model and update itself when necessary. The view will reflect those changes immediately. Angular doesn't include any predefined model type. Instead, we code our models as plain JavaScript and register it as an Angular service. The following code snippet shows the structure of a custom model service Model.js:

```
class Product {
  constructor(){
    this.color = "red";
  }
}
```

The following code snippet shows the structure of ViewModel.js:

```
class ProductController {
  constructor(Product) {
    this.product = Product
  }
}
```

The following code snippet shows the structure of `View.html`:

```
<p>{{ product.color }}</p>
```

Moving from views to components

Angular applications are based around the concept of views. A view in Angular refers to a template (HTML), which is, most of the time, managed by one or more controllers. This view can also contain some custom directives that encapsulate some other chunks of HTML and JavaScript. Naturally, over the years, Angular developers tend to create more and more directives and use them as building blocks that replace the original HTML tags with custom elements.

The concept of composing a view from small custom elements has become trendy and can be found in other popular modern frameworks such as react and polymer. Angular 2 builds around this concept well and will base the UI architecture on those building blocks. Hence from now on, we call components as building blocks and templates as layouts.

Defining components

Components are a clean way of organizing UI code into self-contained, reusable chunks, which contain their own view and logic. Components can be composed together to create a complex user interface. Components can optionally receive properties from the outside world and optionally communicate through callbacks or events. The business logic, structure and styling can be encapsulated inside the component code.

Components in Angular 2 are just directives with a view. Actually, the component in Angular 2 is a type of directive. We can also write a directive that doesn't include a template (and will not be called component) in Angular 2.

Those directives are very similar to the directives you're familiar with in Angular 1.x. The main difference is that in Angular 2.0 we think of two kinds of directives: attribute directives that add behavior to the elements, and structural directives which we named: components.

Breaking the application into components

The angular 2 application is a set of components. We define a component for every UI element, view and route. We must define a root component that we will use as a container for all other components. In other words, an Angular 2 application is a tree of components.

The key for a well-designed, component-oriented Angular 2 application is to break the UI in to a tree of components successfully. For example, let's talk about a simple mobile to-do list application, which looks like this:

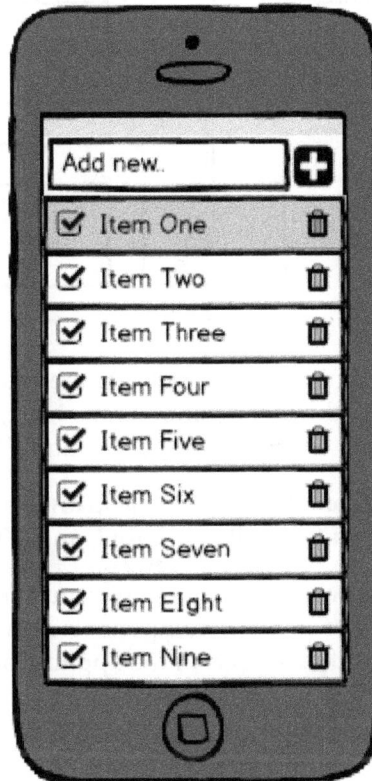

The components tree that composes this UI will look like this:

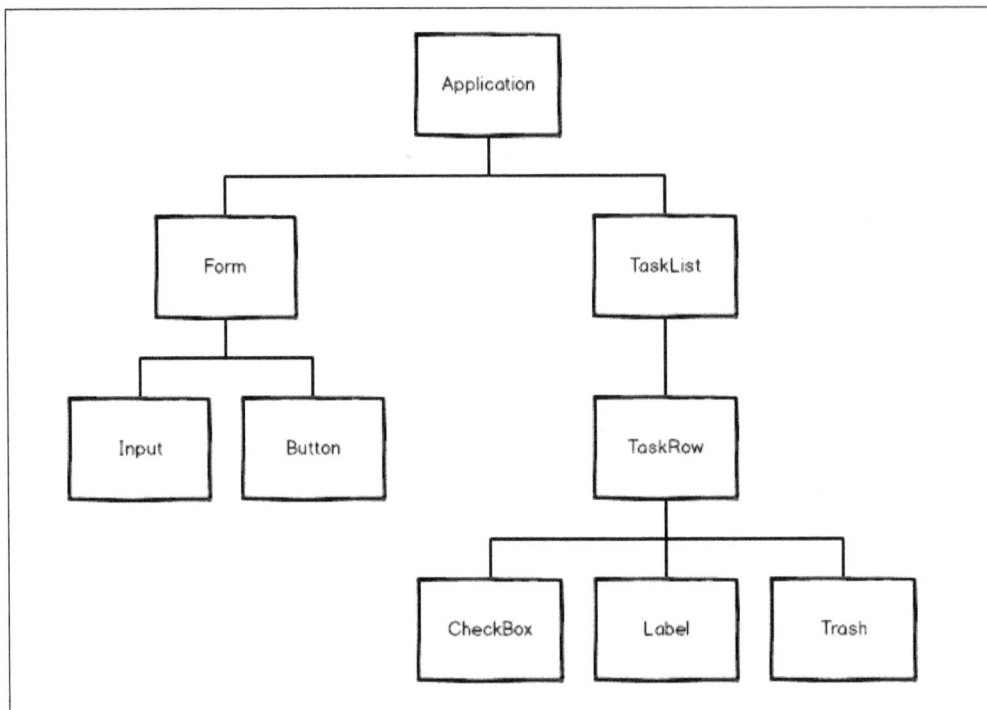

```
                          ┌─────────────┐
                          │ Application │
                          └─────────────┘
              ┌──────────────────┴──────────────────┐
         ┌─────────┐                          ┌─────────┐
         │  Form   │                          │TaskList │
         └─────────┘                          └─────────┘
        ┌─────┴─────┐                               │
   ┌────────┐  ┌────────┐                     ┌──────────┐
   │ Input  │  │ Button │                     │ TaskRow  │
   └────────┘  └────────┘                     └──────────┘
                              ┌────────────────────┼────────────────────┐
                         ┌──────────┐         ┌─────────┐          ┌─────────┐
                         │ CheckBox │         │  Label  │          │  Trash  │
                         └──────────┘         └─────────┘          └─────────┘
```

This application is made up of nine components. At the root is the **Application** component, which contains all the other components. Next, we find the **Form** component, which is built from an **Input** component and a **Button** component.

The **TaskList** component is a container for the **TaskRow** component. Each TaskRow comprises three components—a **CheckBox**, a **Label**, and a **Trash** icon.

There is no strict rule about how many components you should create, but a best practice is to break the UI to as many components as we can. The number of components will affect the other aspects of the application such as reusability, maintenance, and testing.

Summary

The idea of building a UI from components is not new. While in Angular 1 we had the ability to develop directives that act like components, it wasn't mandatory. In Angular 2, the whole application is a tree of components, so the ability to break your design into small parts and learn the how to build components is crucial.

2
Setting Up an Angular 2 Development Environment with angular-cli

Angular 2 takes advantage of modern web technologies and tools, which means the development environment becomes more sophisticated and requires some tools and their understanding.

Luckily, we don't need to spend time installing and configuring all the required dependencies and wiring everything together. We can use the angular-cli (command-line tool) that is being developed in parallel with Angular 2.

In this chapter, we will walk through setting up our development environment with angular-cli: how to install it and how to use it to kickstart our Angular 2 project in minutes.

Node and npm

Before we can start using angular-cli, we need to install Node.js on our machine. Node is a JavaScript runtime built on Chrome's V8 JavaScript engine. It enables JavaScript to run without a browser, which leads to the development of many development tools that we use today, such as task runners, compilers, linters, and module loaders. The modern web frontend development environment relies on these tools.

Installing Node

Node is cross-platform, so it can run on any popular operating system. The easiest way to install `node` is by downloading the official installer for your operating system. To do this, go to `https://nodejs.org/en/` and find the official installer for Windows, Macintosh, or Linux. Currently, Node releases have two major paths—a **Long Time Support** (**LTS**) and a stable version. For this book, we will use the LTS version of Node. Make sure to download the Node 4.24.53 LTS version installer.

After you download and run the installer successfully, open your terminal (or command line in Windows) and type `node -v`. This command should print the current version of `node` that you just installed; in our case, it should be `4.24.53`, or greater.

We use `node` as the JavaScript engine that our development environment tools depend on. The version that was mentioned here does not have any special meaning due to the fact that we won't write any Node.js code throughout this book, but the other tools we use will.

Note! The angular-cli tool will work with any version of node larger than 4.x, so you can use another installation if you like.

Introducing npm

Npm is a package manager for node. It is bundled with the node installer. If you installed `node` successfully in the previous step, npm should be ready to use. To make sure it is installed properly, open the terminal (command line on Windows) and type `npm -v`. This command should print the `npm` version. It should be 3 or greater.

We use `npm` to install the dependencies we need both for development and for runtime. Npm searches for those packages in the `npm` registry, which currently contain more than 1,90,000 packages (and growing). You can either visit `https://www.npmjs.com/` and search for packages, or use the `npm cli` for searching, installing, and managing packages. Npm also helps us manage the project life cycle as we will see next.

Installing angular-cli

We will use npm to install angular-cli on our workstation. To do so, follow these simple steps:

1. Launch the Terminal (or command line in Windows).

2. Type: npm install -g angular-cli@latest and press *Enter* (in Windows, you might need to run this command as an administrator).

That's it! The angular-cli is now installed on your machine, and, because we used the flag -g with our npm install command, angular-cli exposed an ng alias that is available from anywhere. (-g stands for global, which means the module was installed on a system-level directory).

Generating an Angular 2 project

The first command that we will use with angular-cli is new. This command will create a folder structure for our project and install all the required dependencies. Along with the basic Angular 2 files and modules, angular-cli will install modules for testing, linting, and documenting our code. This book is all about components, so we won't touch most of this stuff. You can read more about the available commands on the official angular-cli page: https://cli.angular.io/.

To generate a new project, follow these steps:

1. Launch the Terminal (or command-line in Windows).

2. Type ng new ng_components and press *Enter*.

The angular-cli software will generate a new project under the current directory:

```
                                                   Terminal
templth@kerion ~ $    > ng new ng_components
Could not start watchman; falling back to NodeWatcher for file system events.
Visit http://ember-cli.com/user-guide/#watchman for more info.
installing ng2
  create .editorconfig
  create README.md
  create src/app/app-routing.module.ts
  create src/app/app.component.css
  create src/app/app.component.html
  create src/app/app.component.spec.ts
  create src/app/app.component.ts
  create src/app/app.module.ts
  create src/app/index.ts
  create src/app/shared/index.ts
  create src/assets/.gitkeep
  create src/assets/.npmignore
  create src/environments/environment.prod.ts
  create src/environments/environment.ts
  create src/favicon.ico
  create src/index.html
  create src/main.ts
  create src/polyfills.ts
  create src/styles.css
  create src/test.ts
  create src/tsconfig.json
  create src/typings.d.ts
  create angular-cli.json
  create e2e/app.e2e-spec.ts
  create e2e/app.po.ts
  create e2e/tsconfig.json
  create .gitignore
  create karma.conf.js
  create package.json
  create protractor.conf.js
  create tslint.json
Successfully initialized git.
Installing packages for tooling via npm.
```

Note that the last line prints: Installing packages for tooling via npm. The angular-cli tool will download all the required modules using standard npm command behind the scenes.

That's it! You just generated a complete Angular 2 project with everything you need already configured and wired.

To serve it on top of a development server, follow these steps:

1. Navigate using `cd` into the directory you just created by typing: `cd ng_components`.

2. Type `ng serve` and sit back.

Wait until `angular-cli` prints the following:

```
                                                    Terminal
templte@kerion ~/ng_components $  (master) > ng serve
Could not start watchman; falling back to NodeWatcher for file system events.
Visit http://ember-cli.com/user-guide/#watchman for more info.
** NG Live Development Server is running on http://localhost:4200. **
5867ms building modules
13ms sealing
0ms optimizing
0ms basic module optimization
108ms module optimization
1ms advanced module optimization
9ms basic chunk optimization
0ms chunk optimization
0ms advanced chunk optimization
0ms module and chunk tree optimization
54ms module reviving
2ms module order optimization
3ms module id optimization
3ms chunk reviving
0ms chunk order optimization
9ms chunk id optimization
53ms hashing
1ms module assets processing
118ms chunk assets processing
4ms additional chunk assets processing
0ms recording
0ms additional asset processing
1175ms chunk asset optimization
1240ms asset optimization
28ms emitting
Hash: 196301c55676b67c1ecd
Version: webpack 2.1.0-beta.22
Time: 8707ms
         Asset      Size  Chunks                 Chunk Names
  main.bundle.js   2.83 MB    0, 2  [emitted]  main
 styles.bundle.js  10.2 kB    1, 2  [emitted]  styles
     inline.js     5.53 kB       2  [emitted]  inline
      main.map     2.88 MB    0, 2  [emitted]  main
    styles.map      14 kB    1, 2  [emitted]  styles
    inline.map     5.59 kB       2  [emitted]  inline
    index.html   479 bytes          [emitted]
assets/.npmignore  0 bytes          [emitted]
Child html-webpack-plugin for "index.html":
        Asset    Size  Chunks       Chunk Names
   index.html  2.81 kB       0
webpack: bundle is now VALID.
```

> If you see something related to Brocolli, its because a previous version of `angular-cli` was not properly uninstalled. In such cases, use the following commands:
>
> ```
> $ npm uninstall -g angular-cli
> $ npm cache clean
> ```
>
> Then you can reinstall the tool as described in the chapter, using this command:
>
> ```
> $ npm install -g angular-cli@latest
> ```

Behind the scenes, `angular-cli` builds the project, launches a server and serves the application. All we need to do know is launch our browser and point it to `http://localhost:4200`:

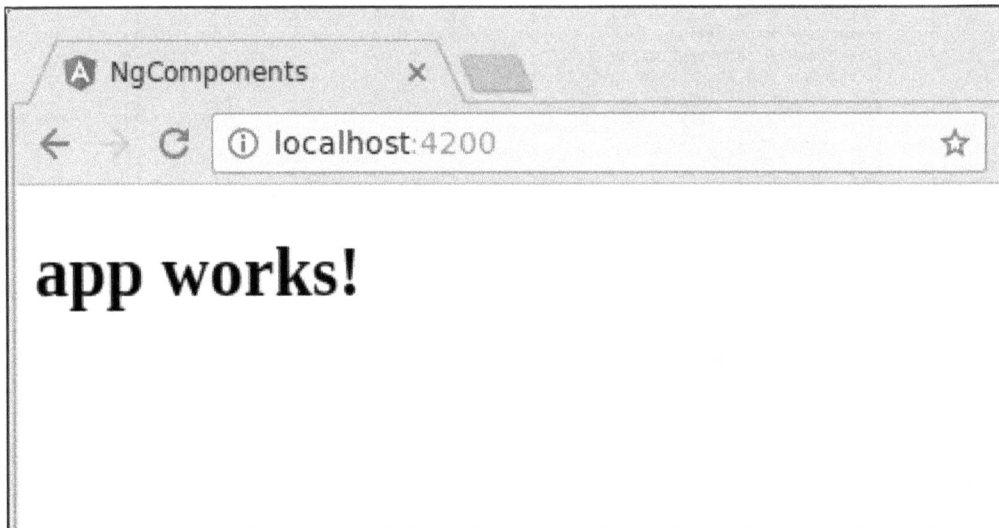

There is a lot going on behind the scenes. The angular-cli tool uses various other tools like `webpack` to perform its magic. These tools are beyond the scope of this book, but you can read all about it in the angular-cli documentation on GitHub at `https://github.com/angular/angular-cli`.

Choosing an IDE

While Angular 2 applications can be developed with a plain text editor, working with an IDE (integrated develop environment) is highly recommended. Personally, I'm using webstorm (https://www.jetbrains.com/webstorm/), which offers complete support for Angular out of the box. If you are looking for a free, open source alternative, we have VSCode (https://code.visualstudio.com/), which also supports Angular 2 naturally. Both of them offer Angular code inspection and highlighting along with refactoring and autocomplete features. WebStorm offers a complete integration with almost every JavaScript tool out there and is considered by many to be the best JavaScript IDE out there.

Summary

In this chapter, we learned how to use angular-cli to create, configure, and serve a new Angular 2 project in minutes. This tool is helping us as developers to focus on our application code rather than on configurations.

In the next chapter, we will get familiar with the TypeScript language, focusing on the important features for building Angular 2 components (and all the rest of the project).

3
The TypeScript Primer

Angular 2 is written with TypeScript, but that doesn't mean we have to write our application with TypeScript. Angular 2 applications can be written with ES6 (JavaScript 2015) or even ES5 (JavaScript 1.5). In this book, we will use TypeScript, mainly (but not only) because of the implementations of decorators, which can clean our Angular 2 code compared to ES6 and ES5.

I will assume that you already know how to write JavaScript 2015 (ES6) code. Through this chapter, we will cover just what we need to know about TypeScript; most of the code is compatible with JavaScript 2015 as is. If you are not familiar with ES6 at all, it's highly recommended to catch up with the new syntax and features.

The following are the topics that we will cover:

- An introduction to the TypeScript language
- Manage dependencies with modules
- Class declarations and usage
- System, built-in, and custom types
- How to use decorators

Introduction to TypeScript

The most important thing that you should know about TypeScript is that it's not a completely new language. It's a superset of ES6. This means an ES6 code can be *converted* to TypeScript just by changing the file extension from `.js` to `.ts`.

For example, the following code is a valid ES6 or TypeScript:

```
class User {
  constructor(id){
     this.id = id;
  }

  getUserInfo(){
     return this.userInfo;
  }
}
```

On the other hand, the TypeScript compiler can target various versions of JavaScript, including ES6. The compiler will peel all the *extra* code and output clean and readable JavaScript code that is almost identical to the source.

This is a simple TypeScript class:

```
class Product {
  private id: number;
  private color: string;

  constructor(id:number, color:string) {
     this.id = id;
     this.color = color;
  }
}
```

Targeting ES6 will output this code:

```
class Product {
  constructor(id, color) {
     this.id = id;
     this.color = color;
  }
}
```

And this is the completion result when targeting ES5:

```
var Product = (function () {
  function Product(id, color) {
     this.id = id;
     this.color = color;
  }
  return Product;
})();
```

As you can see, the compilation results in a clean and readable code, which is almost identical to the source code (in case of ES6).

Next, we will explore the language features. Note that most of the features that we will go through are part of ES6 and not TypeScript. I will mention which feature belongs to TypeScript and which does not.

Managing dependencies with modules

One of the most important changes introduced in JavaScript is modules. A module is a JavaScript file that gets loaded in a special way. All variables and declarations are scoped to the module. If we like to expose some code to the outside world, we need to export it explicitly. If you try to log the value of `this` in the top level of the module, you will get undefined.

The export and import statements

The `export` and `import` keywords are used to define which part of the code should be exposed to other modules, and which code we will like to import from another module. The following module exposes a function, a class, and a variable:

```
[user.ts]
export function getRandomNumber() {
  return Math.random();
}

export class User {
  constructor(name) {
    this.name = name;
  }
}

export const id = 12345;
```

To use this exported code, we need to import it in another module. We can import this code in various ways:

```
// import only the function from the module
import { getRandomNumber } from './user';

// import both the function and the class from the module
import { getRandomNumber, Person } from './user';

// import the function and bind it to a random variable
import { getRandomNumber as random } from './user';
```

```
// import everything from the module and
// bind it to a userModule variable
import * as UserModule from './user';
```

The default exports

We can import only what we need from the module, import multiple code and import everything that the module exported. There is another option to export code from a module, which is called a `default` export:

```
[user.ts]
export default class User {
  constructor(name) {
    this.name = name;
  }
}
```

When importing code that is exported using the default keyword, we don't have to use the exact name of the function or class or variable that we exported:

```
import UserModule from './user.ts';
```

A `default` export can be declared only once per module. We can mix the default and named exports in the same module. Note that we don't have to use curly braces when importing code that has been exported as default.

Classes

The JavaScript language's object-oriented capabilities are built around the concept of prototypes. The prototype model defines links between objects, instead of inheritance trees. The prototype model, as powerful as it is, is not very friendly to the average JavaScript programmer. TypeScript enables us to create classes with a familiar syntax, and it's completely identical to JavaScript 1.5 classes (if we choose not to use TypeScript exclusive features). To define a class in TypeScript, we use the `class` keyword:

```
class Product {}
```

Classes in TypeScript might have a constructor and methods just like JavaScript 2015. TypeScript also adds the ability to define class properties. The following example shows our `Product` class with a constructor, property, and a method:

```
class Product {

  color;
```

```
  price;

  constructor(color, price) {
    this.color = color;
    this.price = price;
  }

  getProductDetails() {
    return this.color + this.price;
  }
}
```

In TypeScript, just like JavaScript 2015, inheritance is achieved through the `extends` keyword, and the `super` keyword is used to call the parent class when necessary. The following example illustrates how to use it:

```
class Product {
  color;
  price;

  constructor(color, price) {
    this.color = color;
    this.price = price;
  }

  getProductDetails() {
    return `${this.color}, ${this.price}`;
  }
}

class Ebook extends Product {
  size;

  constructor(color, price, size) {
    super(color, price);
    this.size = size;
  }

  getProductDetails(){
    return `${this.color}, ${this.price}, ${this.size}`;
  }
}
```

It's important to realize that classes are just a *sugar* on top of prototypes. This means the way JavaScript deals with objects' instantiation and inheritance behind the scenes hasn't changed. It just has a friendly syntax.

In Angular 2, the component that contains all the component behavior is defined as a class. The rest is just a metadata decorator, which we will learn about in the future chapters.

The type system

The most famous feature that made TypeScript what it is, is the type system that enables us to leverage a static type checking at compile time. We have already seen the use of types in the previous code examples. It's important to understand that in TypeScript the use of types is optional but highly recommended. As we saw at the beginning of this chapter, the TypeScript compiler breakdown all the types declaration, so the compilation result will be plain JavaScript.

The basic types

TypeScript supports all the basic JavaScript types you expected: Booleans, Numbers, Strings, and Arrays. The following example shows how to use it in code:

```
// strings
let name: string = "bob";

// boolean
let isLoggedIn: boolean = true;

// number
let height: number = 24;
let width: number = 12;

// arrays
let colors: string[] = ['red', 'green', 'blue'];
let colors: Array<string> = ['red', 'green', 'blue'];
```

TypeScript also includes extra three types to the mix, namely, enum, any, and void. The type any, as the name suggests, is used when we are dealing with dynamic data and we can't tell which type of data we are expecting. If we don't specify a type at all, TypeScript defaults to the any type:

```
// value can be any type, init with a number
let value: any = 10;

// different types can assigned
value = false;
value = "this value is a string";
```

The void type is like the opposite of any. It means *no type*. Most of the time, it is used as a return type for a function that doesn't return:

```
// this function doesn't returns
function setId(id:string): void {
   this.id = id;
}
```

An enum is just a way of giving more friendly names to sets of numeric values. Nothing more. The default numbering starts with 0, and can be set manually to any other numeric value:

```
// default behavior, value of color will be 2;
enum Color {Red, Green, Blue}
let color: Color = Color.Blue;

// manual initialize, value of color will be 6;
enum Color {Red = 2, Green = 4, Blue = 6}
let color: Color = Color.Blue;
```

The custom types

Besides the built-in basic types, you can (and you probably will) use your own types for code that you have written. There are three ways in TypeScript to define types, namely, creating a class, defining an interface, and using special files that declare types for an existing library.

An interface in TypeScript can be described as the *shape* of the object, and usually includes class members and methods without implementation. Interfaces are only at design time; for example, you can't use it as type when defining providers.

The following example illustrates how to use your own classes as types:

```
class Model {}
class Account extends Model {}
class Controller {
   model:Model;
   constructor(model:Model) {
      this.model = Model;
   }
}
new Controller(Account);
```

The following example illustrates how to create an interface for defining a type:

```
interface Model {
   get(query:string): any[];
```

```
  }

  class Account implements Model {
    get(query:string):any[] {
      return [];
    }
  }

  class Controller {
   model:Model;
   constructor(model:Model) {
    this.model = Model;
   }
  }
```

The third option is to create a file with a `.d.ts` extension, which maps an existing code (third party) to types. The process of creating this file is behind the scope of this book, and you can visit `http://www.typescriptlang.org/Handbook#writing-dts-files` to learn more about it.

The good news is that you can find the Definition map for almost any library out there (including Angular). Visit `https://github.com/typings/typings` where you can browse for repositories of Definition maps, and learn more about typings, which is a command-line tool for managing those maps.

About generics

There is another feature that is related to types and that should be mentioned, called *generics*. This feature enables us to create a component that can work over a variety of types rather than a single one.

The generics API is out of the scope of this book, and we won't use this feature through our code example. You can learn more about generics by visiting `http://www.typescriptlang.org/Handbook#generics`.

Using decorators

Decorators are functions that modify a class, property, method, or method parameter. The following example illustrates how to define and use a simple decorator that adds a static parameter to the class:

```
// decorator function
function AddMetadata (...args) {
  return function (target){
    target.metadata = [...args];
  }
```

```
}

// decorator applied
@AddMetadata({ metadata: 'some values'})
class Model {
}
```

The three dots syntax (. . .) is the *spread operator,* which is a feature of JavaScript 2015 that deconstructs the items of a given array.

Decorators versus annotations

You might have heard the term annotations; they are simply metadata related to Angular 2. Before the Angular team decided to use TypeScript, they introduced us to a new language that they called AtScript. This language included a feature called annotations, which look exactly like decorators. So what's the difference? The decorator is an interface for creating those Angular annotations. Decorators are executed and in Angular 2, they have the responsibility to set metadata leveraging the Reflect Metadata library. Furthermore, decorators are a proposal for ES7 — the next version of JavaScript. For that reason, we can focus on decorators.

Summary

TypeScript is a superset of JavaScript. This means you can write plain JavaScript in .ts files. The TypeScript compiler will peel all the extra TypeScript code and produce code that is plain, readable, and almost identical to the source code. The Angular 2 team uses TypeScript for developing the Angular platform (the source code is written with TypeScript, but a compiled JavaScript version is also available). As developers, we can choose whatever we want to use; TypeScript, JavaScript 2015 (ES6), or JavaScript 1.5.

If you choose to use TypeScript, it's highly recommended to visit http://www.typescriptlang.org/ and learn more about the language's capabilities that go beyond the scope of this book.

4
Building a Basic Component

At its core, an Angular 2 component is a class that is responsible for exposing data to the view and implementing user interaction logic. An Angular 2 component can be compared to the controller, scope, and view of Angular 1.

How does Angular 2 know how to treat our class as a component? We need to attach metadata to the class to tell Angular how to treat it.

The term metadata describes the additional information that we add to our code. This information is used by Angular 2 at runtime.

In this chapter, we will cover the following topics:

- The anatomy of an Angular 2 component
- The component selector
- Component template
- Component style
- View encapsulation (the shadow DOM)
- Data binding
- Anatomy of an Angular 2 component

In *Chapter 2, Setting Up an Angular 2 Development Environment with angular-cli*, setting the development environment, we generated an Angular 2 project from scratch using the `angular-cli` tool and served it to the browser. If you haven't done so, refer to *Chapter 2, Setting Up an Angular 2 Development Environment with angular-cli*, and follow the steps.

After you are done, it's time to open the project in our favorite IDE (also described in *Chapter 2, Setting Up an Angular 2 Development Environment with angular-cli*), to inspect the code. It should be similar to the following screenshot:

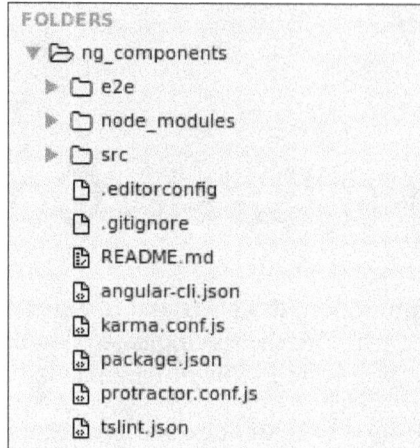

```
FOLDERS
▼ 🗁 ng_components
  ▶ 🗀 e2e
  ▶ 🗀 node_modules
  ▶ 🗀 src
    🗋 .editorconfig
    🗋 .gitignore
    📄 README.md
    🗋 angular-cli.json
    🗋 karma.conf.js
    🗋 package.json
    🗋 protractor.conf.js
    🗋 tslint.json
```

When we generate our project using `angular-cli`, a component with our application name (that we supplied to the `ng new` command) is created for us. We can find it under the `src/app` directory as follows:

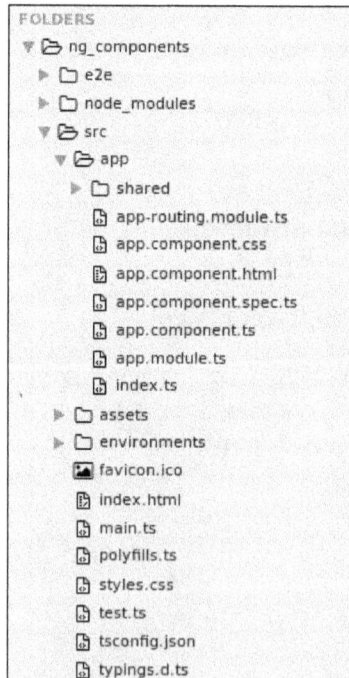

```
FOLDERS
▼ 🗁 ng_components
  ▶ 🗀 e2e
  ▶ 🗀 node_modules
  ▼ 🗁 src
    ▼ 🗁 app
      ▶ 🗀 shared
        🗋 app-routing.module.ts
        🗋 app.component.css
        📄 app.component.html
        🗋 app.component.spec.ts
        🗋 app.component.ts
        🗋 app.module.ts
        🗋 index.ts
    ▶ 🗀 assets
    ▶ 🗀 environments
      🖼 favicon.ico
      📄 index.html
      🗋 main.ts
      🗋 polyfills.ts
      🗋 styles.css
      🗋 test.ts
      🗋 tsconfig.json
      🗋 typings.d.ts
```

Locate the file named `app.component.ts` and open it in the editing view (the editing view can be differ from one IDE to another).

Let's explore the component code line by line, here is the code of `app.component.ts`

```
[app.component.ts]
import { Component } from '@angular/core';

@Component({
    selector: 'app-root',
    templateUrl: './app.component.html',
    styleUrls: ['./app.component.css']
})
export class AppComponent {
    title = 'app works!';
}
```

In the first line, we are importing the `Component` decorator from the Angular core module

- Then, we declare the `Component` decorator by assigning the @ symbol following the name of the decorator. Because the decorator is just a function (refer to *Chapter 3, The TypeScript Primer* for an explanation), we need to invoke it just like any other function using parenthesis.

- The `Component` decorator accepts an object as a parameter, which defines the component metadata. We will explore it in a second.

- Right after the decorator, we declare the component class, which should hold our component logic and currently declares the string named `title`

- The class needs to be exported so it can be used in other places in the code

As we can see, Angular 2 components must be built from two distinct parts: a simple class and a decorator.

Before we dive into this code, let's open the browser and explore the elements that have been rendered to the browser.

To do so, point your browser to http://localhost:4200/ (I'm using Google Chrome), right-click on the title and choose **Inspect** from the pop-up menu:

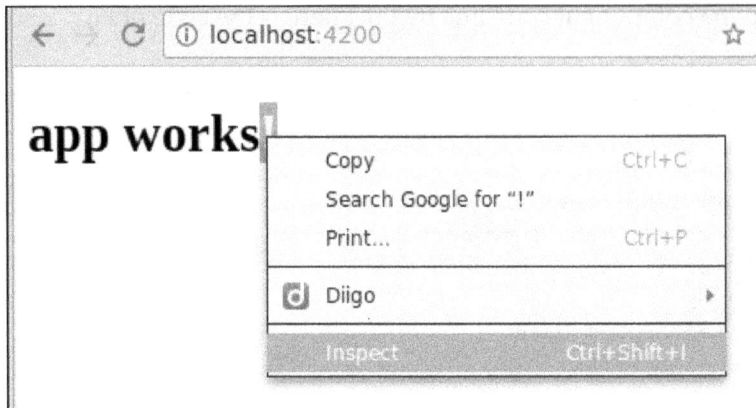

This will open up the Chrome DevTool where we will explore the DOM:

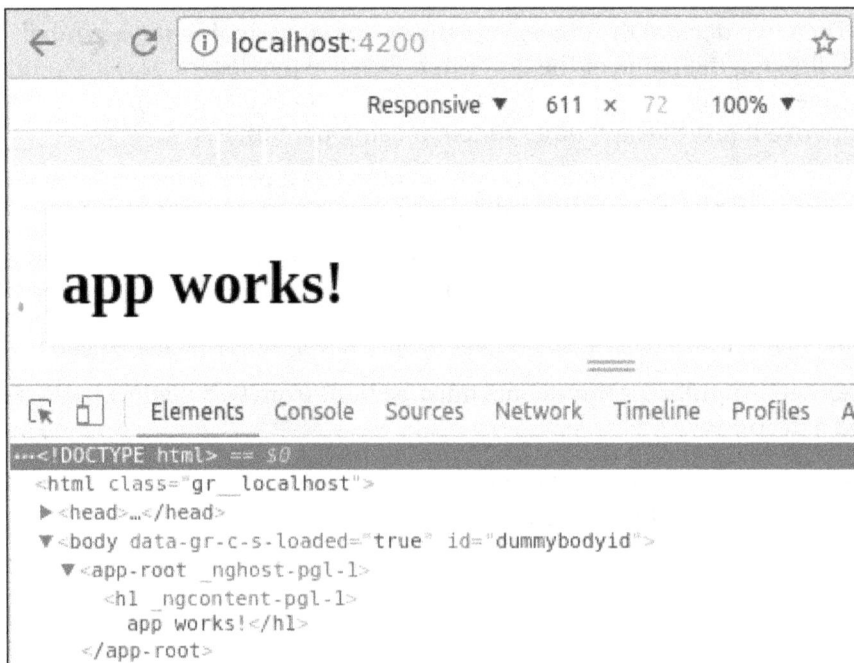

The selector that we defined in our metadata becomes an element with the same name, and the title that we defined on the component class is rendered as an <h1> tag inside it.

How has the `<app-root>` found its way to the DOM? Where does that `<h1>` tag come from?

Bootstrapping the application

Before dealing with how the link is made between components and the DOM, let's introduce the concept of module and how it's used to bootstrap the application.

Under the `src` directory in the project root, locate and open the `main.ts` file:

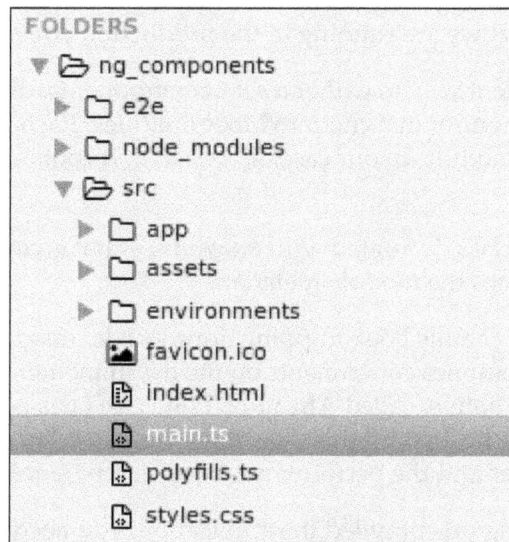

```
FOLDERS
 ▼ 🗁 ng_components
    ▶ 🗀 e2e
    ▶ 🗀 node_modules
    ▼ 🗁 src
       ▶ 🗀 app
       ▶ 🗀 assets
       ▶ 🗀 environments
         🖼 favicon.ico
         📄 index.html
         📄 main.ts
         📄 polyfills.ts
         📄 styles.css
```

This file is the starting point of our Angular application. It is responsible for instantiating the main module of the application and the root component in it. To do so, we import a `platformBrowserDynamic` method from the `platform-browser-dynamic` module, which is a part of Angular. This method returns an object to bootstrap the application. The `bootstrapModule` method of this object is responsible for kicking off Angular by rendering the root component of the component tree. It requires the main module to be passed as an argument, so we import our module class `AppModule` and pass it to `bootstrap`:

The following code is from the `main.ts` file:

```
import './polyfills.ts';
import { platformBrowserDynamic } from '@angular/platform-browser-
dynamic';
import { enableProdMode } from '@angular/core';
import { environment } from './environments/environment';
```

```
import { AppModule } from './app/';

if (environment.production) {
  enableProdMode();
}


platformBrowserDynamic().bootstrapModule(AppModule);
```

The rest of the code doesn't have any effect on bootstrapping Angular with a root module. The `enableProdMode` method is a method from Angular core that runs the application in production mode. The environment is just a constant that holds a Boolean that indicates if we are running in the production environment.

Modules are a convenient way to gather a set of components, directives, services and pipes into a single entity that can into other modules. Each Angular application contains a single root module, in our case, `AppModule`. It contains the root component of the application.

A module is simply a class decorated with `@NgModule` that accepts an object as a parameter, which defines the module metadata.

Note that we use the dynamic bootstrapping approach leveraging the Just-in-Time compiler. This compiles components on the fly, in memory, and in the browser. Another alternative, called **Ahead of Time (AoT)**, is possible in Angular 2 to precompile the application. In this case, there is no need to ship the Angular compiler to the browser and the performance boost can be significant.

In this case, after having precompiled the application, you need to use the `platformBrowserDynamic` method from the `platform-browser-dynamic` module for the `main.ts` file:

```
import './polyfills.ts';
import { platformBrowser } from '@angular/platform-browser';
import { enableProdMode } from '@angular/core';
import { environment } from './environments/environment';
import { AppModuleNgFactory } from './app/app.module.ng.factory';

if (environment.production) {
  enableProdMode();

}


platformBrowser().bootstrapModuleFactory(AppModuleNgFactory);
```

The component selector

As we have seen in the first example of this chapter, the **selector** that we defined in the component decorator becomes an element that renders to the DOM. Before we explore our selector options, let's understand how Angular renders this component.

As we discussed in *Chapter 1, Angular 2 Component Architecture*, an Angular 2 application can be described as a tree of components. Like any other tree structure, there is only one root node. Currently in our project we got only one component, which is used as the tree node.

With this information, let's see how Angular instantiates our root component and renders it:

Under the src/app directory in the project root, locate and open the app.module.ts file. This file contains the definition of the root module of the application:

```
[app.module.ts]
import { BrowserModule } from '@angular/platform-browser';
import { NgModule } from '@angular/core';
import { FormsModule } from '@angular/forms';
import { HttpModule } from '@angular/http';
import { AppComponent } from './app.component';

@NgModule({
  declarations: [
    AppComponent
  ],

  imports: [
    BrowserModule,
    FormsModule,
    HttpModule
  ],

  providers: [],
  bootstrap: [AppComponent]
})
export class AppModule { }
```

The app.module.ts is responsible for instantiating the component class. When this happens, Angular searches for the selector that we defined in the component decorator in the index.html file. The only component that we need to place inside our index.html is our root component defined in the bootstrap attribute of the root module in the app.module.ts.

Note that this component needs to be specified in the `declarations` attribute listing all usable components for the module.

Open `index.html` which is located next to `main.ts` and inspect the code:

```
[index.html]
<html>
  <head>
    <!-- other code related to the page head -->
  </head>
  <body>
    <app-root>Loading...</app-root>
  </body>
</html>
```

The first thing we see is that we used our selector as element in our `html` file. This is the default behavior of Angular.

The other code that you find in `index.html` is related to the build system that `angular-cli` uses, which is out of the scope of this book.

All you need to know is that when this HTML is loaded into the server, all the required dependencies are loaded for Angular and you need to run the code in `main.ts` to kickstart the framework.

Selector options

When we build components, we are creating new html elements. That's the reason that, by default, our selector name is used as an element in the HTML. But we have other options as well for building components. Let's explore them:

- Select by CSS class name:

```
@Component({
  selector: '.app-root'
})
```

  Use in markup:

```
<div class="app-root">Loading...</div>
```

- Select by attribute name:

```
@Component({
  selector: '[app-root]'
})
```

Use in markup:

```
<div app-root>Loading...</div>
```

- Select by attribute name and value:

```
@Component({
  selector: 'div[app=components]'
})
```

Use in markup:

```
<div app="components">Loading...</div>
```

- Select only if the element does not match the selector:

```
@Component({
  selector: 'div:not(.widget)'
})
```

Use in markup:

```
<div class="app">Loading...</div>
```

- Select if one of the selectors matches:

```
@Component({
  selector: 'app-root, .app, [ng=app]'
})
```

Use in markup:

```
<app-root>Loading...</app-root>
<div class="app">Loading...</div>
<div ng="app">Loading...</div>
```

Most of the time, leaving the default—which is the component selector—is exactly what we want when building common components. In the later chapters, we will see other usages as well.

For now, we will leave the selector as default.

The component template

The template is the heart of the component in Angular 2. Without a template there is nothing to render to the DOM. There are two ways to attach a template to the component:

- Providing a URL to an external html file
- Define the template inline

The `app-root` that is created by the `angular-cli` includes an external template. It is defined with the `templateUrl` property:

```
[app.component.ts]
@Component({
  selector: 'app-root',
  templateUrl: './app.component.html'
})
```

We can find the template next to `app.component.ts` as an HTML file with the same name `app.component.html`. Let's open it to inspect the code:

```
[app.component.html]
<h1>
  {{title}}
</h1>
```

Now we know where the `<h1>` came from. As you can guess, the double curly braces render the title from the component class.

If we want to declare our templates inline, we should use the template property instead. Luckily, in ES6, we are introduce with a way to create multiline strings easily. This feature is called **template strings** and it's declared with the back tick (`` ` ``) character. In the following example, we demonstrate how to declare an inline template:

```
[app.component.ts]
@Component({
  selector: 'app-root',
  template: `
    <h1>
      {{title}}
    </h1>

  `
})
```

Keeping the template inline is comfortable as we can see both the template and the component class in the same file.

Embedding styles in component template

We will probably want to use some CSS in our component's template. Like templates, we have two options—specifying our CSS classes inline or supplying a URL for external style sheets. Currently, our component uses one external CSS file, by declaring a path in the `styleUrls` array.

As the property name suggests, we can supply more than one URL to pull the CSS from. The styles defined on those CSS files are now available for use within our template. First let's take a look at the current component declaration:

```
[app.component.ts]
@Component({
  selector: 'app-root',
  template: `
    <h1>
      {{title}}
    </h1>
  `,
  styleUrls: ['./app.component.css']
})
```

Alternatively, we can define styles inline, just like the template, by using the **styles** property instead. **styles** is an array of strings where we can write our CSS rules. The following example demonstrates how to style the `<h1>` tag using inline styles:

```
[app.component.ts]
@Component({
  selector: 'app-root',
  template: `
    <h1>
      {{title}}
    </h1>
  `,
  styles: [`
    h1 { color: darkblue }
  `]
})
```

Let's explore the element in Chrome DevTool. Right-click on the `title` and choose inspect from the pop up menu. The Chrome DevTool will launch:

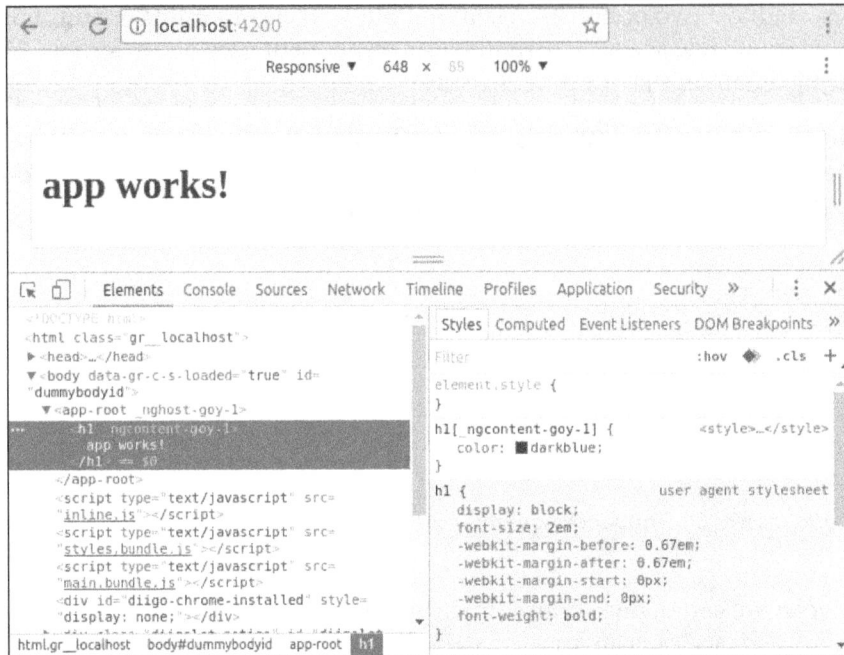

Looking at the element through the DevTool, we expose some facts about component styling:

- The style that we defined is transformed into an inline style tag on the `head` section on top of the `html` document
- The style definition is changed and now includes a property next to it, which makes it specific and almost impossible to override

Angular protects the component styling from overriding by generating a unique property and attaches it to the original CSS selector that we defined. This behavior tries to mimic the way that the shadow DOM works. So, before we can move forward, we need to understand what the shadow DOM is.

The shadow DOM

When we are creating a component in Angular 2, a shadow DOM is created and our template gets loaded into it (not by default). What is a shadow DOM? Shadow DOM refers to a subtree of DOM elements that renders as part of the document, but not into the main document DOM tree.

Let's see a well-known example of a shadow DOM, an HTML `select`, in action. Create a plain HTML file in your favorite text editor and create a `select` element in its body:

```
<!doctype html>
<html lang="en">
  <head>
    <meta charset="UTF-8">
    <title>Document</title>
  </head>
  <body>
    <select>
      <option>ONE</option>
      <option>TWO</option>
      <option>THREE</option>
    </select>
  </body>
</html>
```

Next, open it up in Chrome and right-click on the element, then choose **Inspect Element** from the pop-up menu:

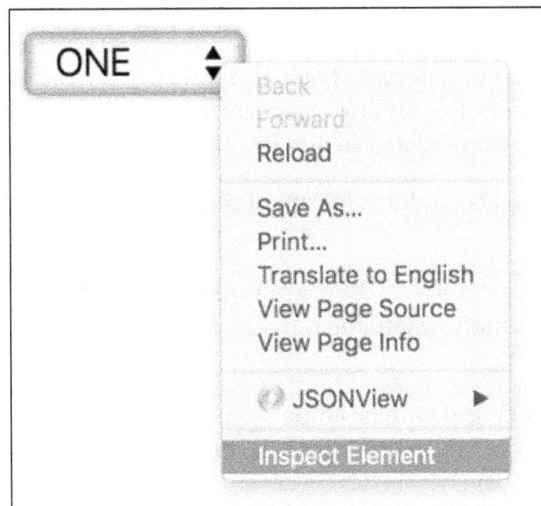

The Chrome DevTool will pop up, and we can inspect the select element in the **Elements** tab:

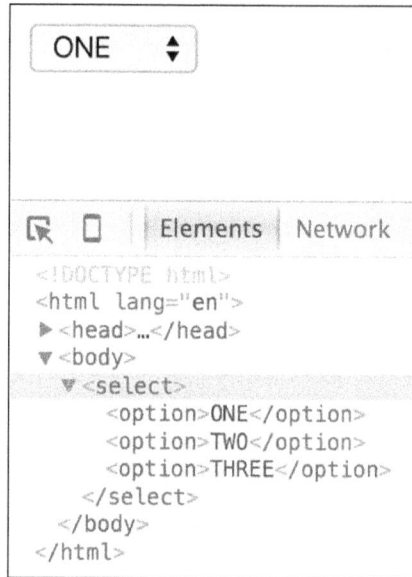

If you have ever tried to customize the appearance of a native html select element with CSS, you know that you need to hack and develop a workaround to make it work. The select element has styling structure, and even a built-in behavior, but we can't see it. It's encapsulated inside the element.

If you are not familiar with the term encapsulation here is a quick definition taken from Wikipedia:

Encapsulation is an Object Oriented Programming concept that binds together the data and functions that manipulate the data, and that keeps both safe from outside interference and misuse.

So, where does the select appearance come from? Chrome DevTool has a feature that can rival the shadow DOM of this element. To enable this, go to the Settings menu of Chrome DevTool:

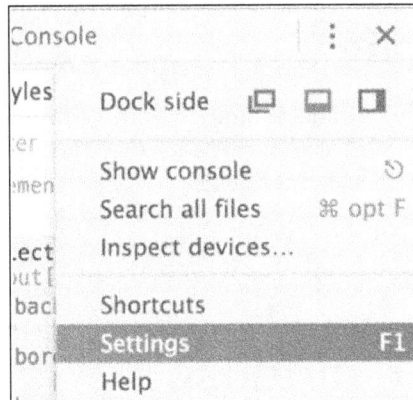

Scroll down and find the **Elements** section. Check the checkbox **Show user agent shadow DOM**:

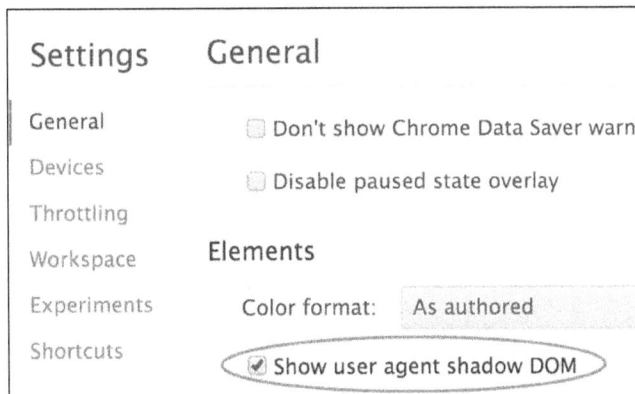

Now, let's inspect the `select` element again:

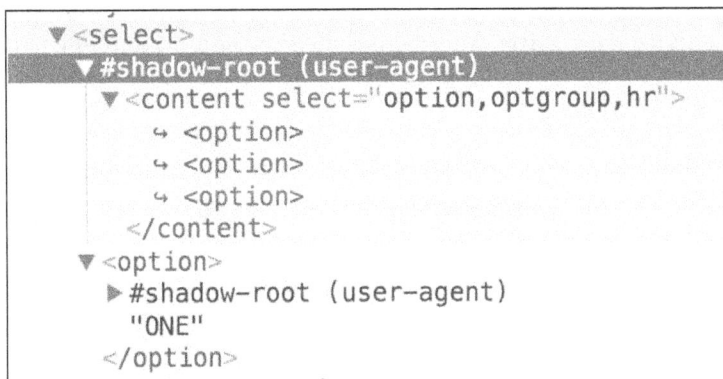

Now we clearly see that the `select` element hides a secret DOM tree. Under the `select` element, a new root is created (the `#shadow-root`) and a content element renders right under it. The hidden content tag has an attribute called `select`, which defines some internal behavior. This is same for the option tag. If you would like to explore one more popular HTML element that creates a shadow DOM, you can repeat those steps using `<input type='file' />`.

This powerful ability to create a native element, which encapsulates its own styling, behavior, and even data, is also possible with Angular 2.

Encapsulation modes

By default, as we have seen, our component won't encapsulate its structure and styling. This means that CSS classes from outside of the component can override and affect the embedded CSS styles that we defined, and the HTML structure of the component is accessible as well.

Angular will generate a unique property for our `selector` to protect our styling, but this can be overridden with a CSS `!important` statement.

To change this, we need to define an encapsulation mode. Angular 2 provides us three options to choose from:

- **Emulated** (the default): Angular will add a special attribute to the class `selector` to avoid affecting other styles outside of the components.

- **Native**: This is the native encapsulation mechanism of the renderer that will be applied. In our case, it's the browser. Angular will create a shadow DOM for this component, which means that external CSS can't affect our component.

- **None**: No encapsulation will be applied.

To define encapsulation options, we need to import the `ViewEncapsulation` from Angular core and use one of the options to define the component encapsulation property. The following example demonstrates how to set the component encapsulation model to `None`:

```
[app.component.ts]
@Component({
  selector: 'app-root',
  encapsulation: ViewEncapsulation.None,
  template: `
    <h1>
      {{title}}
    </h1>
```

```
  `,
  styles: [`
    h1 { color: darkblue }
  `]
})
```

Most of the time, leaving the default emulate mode is fine. In the future chapters, we will encounter some situations where setting the mode to None is crucial.

Data bindings

To fully understand the component code that was generated for us by angular-cli, we need to talk about data bindings. In other words, the way that we were able to render the **title** declared on the component class to component template.

First, let's take a look at the entire component code:

```
[app.component.ts]
import { Component, ViewEncapsulation } from '@angular/core';

@Component({
  selector: 'app-root',
  encapsulation: ViewEncapsulation.None,
  template: `
    <h1>
      {{title}}
    </h1>
  `,
  styles: [`
    h1 { color: darkblue }
  `]
})
export class AppComponent {
  title = 'app works!';
}
```

It's not hard to spot the double curly braces in the template. This is a part of Angular's template syntax, which is responsible for one way binding of data from the component class. In this case, we are binding the title property (which is a string) to be rendered between the <h1> tag.

Later in this book, we will explore some more binding options.

Summary

In Angular 2, a component is a class with a decorator that adds important metadata to it. The component decorator defines how we can use it, and what it can do. The selector and the template are the minimum required fields when calling the decorator (Angular will throw an error if one of them is missing).

If we defined the view encapsulation as native, Angular will create a shadow DOM for our component, which protects the embedded styles from being affected by external CSS on the page.

In the next chapter, we will continue to develop our component and make it dynamic.

5
Building Dynamic Components

Components are data driven by nature. They should be able to render dynamic data, respond to user interactions, and react to events.

In this chapter, we will continue where we stopped in *Chapter 4*, *Building a Basic Component*, focusing on the component template syntax, and learn how to bind data and events.

The topics that will be covered are as follows:

- Data interpolation
- Using core directives
- Properties binding
- Events bindings
- Two-way bindings

Data interpolation

In *Chapter 3*, *The TypeScript Primer*, we bound a simple string to the template. If you haven't done it, refer to *Chapter 4*, *Building a Basic Component*. Let's overview our app-component code:

```
[app.component.ts]
import { Component, ViewEncapsulation } from '@angular/core';

@Component({
  selector: 'app-root',
  encapsulation: ViewEncapsulation.None,
  template: `
```

```
      <h1>
        {{title}}
      </h1>
      `,
    styles: [`
      h1 { color: darkblue }
      `]
  })
  export class AppComponent {
    title = 'app works!';
  }
```

For now, we will focus on the template. Remove the `encapsulation` and `styles` properties from the component decorator to make it more clear and focused. While doing this, let's add a type and a constructor to our class as well:

```
[app.component.ts]
import { Component } from '@angular/core';

@Component({
  selector: 'app-root',
  template: `
    <h1>
      {{ title }}
    </h1>
    `
})
export class AppComponent {
  title: string;

  constructor() {
    this.title = 'app works!';
  }
}
```

This is a one-way binding from the data source (the component class in our case) to the view (the component template). Angular interpolates the `title` and outputs the result between the double curly brace.

The double curly braces can only interpolate strings. If we try to bind an object, it will not work. In the following example, instead of a `title`, I created an object which contains the `title` and inspects the result in the browser:

```
[app.component.ts]
```

```
import { Component } from '@angular/core';

@Component({
  selector: 'app-root',
  template: `
    <h1>
      {{ info }}
    </h1>
  `
})
export class AppComponent {
  info: {};

  constructor() {
    this.info = {title: 'app works!'};
  }
}
```

Here is the output:

> If you can't see the result in the browser, make sure you run the ng serve command. If you are not sure how to do it, refer to *Chapter 2, Setting Up an Angular 2 Development Environment with angular-cli.*

We can bind to object properties, just remember that everything will be interpolated as a string. The following example will render the title properly:

```
[app.component.ts]
import { Component } from '@angular/core';

@Component({
  selector: 'app-root',
```

```
    template: `
      <h1>
        {{ info.title }}
      </h1>
    `
})
export class AppComponent {
  info: {};

  constructor() {
    this.info = {title: 'app works!'}
  }
}
```

What we write between the curly braces is an angular expression. It means that
angular evaluates the expression before it is converted into a string. In other words,
we can put simple logic in our expressions and even bind to a method. Consider the
following example:

```
[app.component.ts]
import { Component } from '@angular/core';

@Component({
  selector: 'app-root',
  template: `
    <h1>{{ info.title }}</h1>
    <h2>{{ info.subtitle || 'alternative text' }}</h2>
    <h3>My name is: {{ getFullName() }}</h3>
  `
})
export class AppComponent {
  info: {};
  firstName: string;
  lastName: string;

  constructor() {
    this.info = {title: 'app works!'}
    this.firstName = 'Nir';
    this.lastName = 'Kaufman';
  }

  getFullName(){
    return `${this.firstName} ${this.lastName}`;
  }
}
```

Inside angular expressions we can't use the `new` keyword and operators such as: `++`, `--`, and `+=`.

As a rule of thumb, expressions shouldn't be complex.

The context of the component template is the component instance. It means that you can't access global variables such as `window`, `document`, or `console.log`.

Core directives

If you are familiar with Angular 1.x, you already know what a directive is. If not, here is a quick definition: a directive is a custom attribute that adds functionality to an element. In Angular, a component is considered to be a special case of a directive which contains a template.

Angular 2 core includes several directives—NgClass, NgFor, NgIf, NgStyle, NgSwitch, NgSwitchWhen, and NgSwitchDefault.

If you are familiar with Angular 1, you already know what these directives can do, although the syntax and the underneath implementation have been changed.

Those directives aim to help us implement common templating tasks such as DOM manipulation.

To be able to use core directives in a component, we need to import the `BrowserModule` module into the module where the component fits. This was automatically done by angular-cli when generating the application within the `app.module.ts` file:

```typescript
import { BrowserModule } from '@angular/platform-browser';
import { NgModule } from '@angular/core';
import { AppComponent } from './app.component';

@NgModule({
  declarations: [
    AppComponent
  ],

  imports: [
    BrowserModule
  ],

  bootstrap: [AppComponent]
})
export class AppModule { }
```

Let's explore how to use them in our code.

NgIf

Just like Angular 1, the NgIf directive will remove or recreate a portion of the DOM based on an expression that we passed. The expression should evaluate to `true` or `false`.

Here is how we use `ngIf`:

```
[app.component.ts]
import { Component } from '@angular/core';

@Component({
  selector: 'app-root',
  template: `
    <h1>{{ info.title }}</h1>
    <h2>{{ info.subtitle || 'alternative text' }}</h2>
    <h3 *ngIf="showFullName">My name is: {{ getFullName() }}</h3>
  `
})
export class AppComponent {
  info: {};
  firstName: string;
  lastName: string;
  showFullName: boolean;

  constructor() {
    this.info = {title: 'app works!'};
    this.firstName = 'Nir';
    this.lastName = 'Kaufman';
    this.showFullName = false;
  }

  getFullName(){
    return `${this.firstName} ${this.lastName}`;
  }
}
```

Don't worry about the asterisk before the `ngIf` attribute, we will discuss it in a moment. We assign an expression called `showFullName`, which exists on the component class. So, on the component class, we declare a class member called `showFullName` of type Boolean and initialize it on the constructor to be `false`.

As a result, the `<h3>` tag will not render to the DOM, and we won't see the full name.

The asterisk – *

The asterisk (*) before the directive name is a syntactic sugar of Angular that hides the use of the `<template>` tag from us. This tag is being used in *structural directives*, which is a term that describes a directive that impacts the structure of the DOM.

The preceding example can be written like this:

```
[app.component.ts]
import { Component } from '@angular/core';

@Component({
  selector: 'app-root',
  template: `
    <h1>{{ info.title }}</h1>
    <h2>{{ info.subtitle || 'alternative text' }}</h2>

      <template [ngIf]="showFullName">
        <h3>My name is: {{ getFullName() }}</h3>
      </template>
  `
})
export class AppComponent {
  info: {};
  firstName: string;
  lastName: string;
  showFullName: boolean;

  constructor() {
    this.info = {title: 'app works!'};
    this.firstName = 'Nir';
    this.lastName = 'Kaufman';
    this.showFullName = false;
  }

  getFullName(){
    return `${this.firstName} ${this.lastName}`;
  }
}
```

That's what Angular will do behind the scenes, but we don't need to worry when using the shorter version of the syntax.

NgClass

The NgClass directive, just like in Angular 1, conditionally adds and removes CSS classes. We pass an expression that can be interpreted in three different ways:

- A string that contains all the CSS classes that we want to add, delimited by space

- An array of CSS classes to be added

- An object that maps CSS classes to a Boolean value (`true` or `false`)

Let's demonstrate the various options to use `ngClass`, start with a string:

```
[app.component.ts]
import { Component } from '@angular/core';

@Component({
  selector: 'app-root',
  styles: [`
    .italic { font-style: italic}
    .info { color: blue; }
  `],
  template: `
    <h1>{{ info.title }}</h1>
    <h2 [ngClass]="getClass()">
      {{ info.subtitle || 'alternative text' }}</h2>

    <template [ngIf]="showFullName">
      <h3>My name is: {{ getFullName() }}</h3>
    </template>
  `
})
export class AppComponent {
  info: {};
  firstName: string;
  lastName: string;
  showFullName: boolean;

  constructor() {
    this.info = {title: 'app works!'};
    this.firstName = 'Nir';
    this.lastName = 'Kaufman';
    this.showFullName = false;
  }
```

```
getFullName(){
   return `${this.firstName} ${this.lastName}`;
}

getClass(){
   return 'info italic';
}
}
```

We apply the ngClass to the <h2> tag and pass a method that we implement on the component class. The getClass() method returns a string containing a string that includes the names of both of the CSS classes we want to append to the <h2> element. Don't worry about the square brackets that surround the ngClass directive. We will explain this syntax in a moment.

We could implement that method in two other ways in order to achieve the same result:

- The first is by returning an array:

```
getClass(){
   return ['info', 'italic'];
}
```

Returning an object:

```
getClass(){
   return { italic: true, info: true };
}
```

- The second is by using square brackets ([ ])

> In Angular 2, we can bind data directly to DOM or directive properties. The ngClass selector was defined as a property, so if we want to use it, we need to use the square brackets syntax. We will see more examples later in this chapter when we deal with data bindings.

NgStyle

The ngStyle directive will change the inline styles of the element based on an expression that evaluates an object. In the following example, we will use ngStyle to dynamically assign a font size to the title:

```
[app.component.ts]
import { Component } from '@angular/core';
```

```
@Component({
  selector: 'app-root',
  styles: [`
    .italic { font-style: italic}
    .info { color: blue; }
  `],
  template: `
    <h1 [ngStyle]="{'font-size': titleSize }">{{ info.title }}</h1>
    <h2 [ngClass]="getClass()">
      {{ info.subtitle || 'alternative text' }}</h2>

    <template [ngIf]="showFullName">
      <h3>My name is: {{ getFullName() }}</h3>
    </template>
  `
})
export class AppComponent {
  info: {};
  firstName: string;
  lastName: string;
  showFullName: boolean;
  titleSize: string;

  constructor() {
    this.info = {title: 'app works!'};
    this.firstName = 'Nir';
    this.lastName = 'Kaufman';
    this.showFullName = false;
    this.titleSize = '96px';
  }

  getFullName() {
    return `${this.firstName} ${this.lastName}`;
  }

  getClass() {
    return { italic: true, info: true };
  }
}
```

In this example, we created a class member that initializes a property named titleSize and then uses it to determine the font size style on the <h1> tag, with ngStyle.

NgSwitch

The NgSwitch directive adds or removes DOM subtrees according to the value of the `switch` expression. To effectively use this directive, we used `ngSwitchCase` and `ngSwitchDefault` within the `ngSwitch` directive block:

```
<div [ngSwitch]="cases">
  <div *ngSwitchCase="1">Case 1</div>
  <div *ngSwitchCase="2">Case 2</div>
  <div *ngSwitchDefault>Default Case</div>
</div>
```

There are a few things to notice—the `ngSwitch` directive is not a structural directive, which means it does not use a `<template>` tag and also does not manipulate the DOM tree. This is done by the `ngSwitchCase` and the `ngSwitchDefault` directives. So, we use the square brackets when using the `ngSwitch` directive, and the asterisk for the rest.

NgFor

The `ngFor` directive creates a new element (instantiates a new template), once per item from a collection that it repeats. If you are familiar with Angular 1, the `ngFor` directive is similar to the `ng-repeat` directive in concept, but the underneath implementation and syntax is different:

In the following example, we are creating a list of colors by repeating each element in a string array:

```
@Component({
  selector: 'app-root',
  template: `
    <ul>
      <li *ngFor="let color of colors">{{ color }}</li>
    </ul>
  `
})
export class AppComponent {
  colors: string[] = ['red', 'green', 'blue'];
}
```

Property bindings

With Angular 2, we can easily bind to each DOM property. For example, let's bind a value to the `disabled` property of a button and initialize it to be `true`:

```
@Component({
  selector: 'app-root',
  template: `
   <button [disabled]="isDisabled">You can't click me!</button>
  `
})
export class AppComponent {
  private isDisabled: boolean;

  constructor() {
    this.isDisabled = true;
  }
}
```

This is true to any property. Let's see another example, this time with an input element:

```
@Component({
  selector: 'app-root',
  template: `
    <input [type]="inputType" [placeholder]="placeHolderText">
  `
})
export class AppComponent {
  private placeHolderText: string;
  private inputType: string;
  private inputClass: string;

  constructor() {
    this.placeHolderText = 'type your password...'
    this.inputType = 'password';
  }
}
```

Event bindings

Up until now, we learned about two kinds of data binding: interpolation (using the curly braces) and properties binding. Both of them are considered to be one-way data binding from the data source to the view. In real life, our component should be able to respond to user events. Luckily, in Angular 2, this is simple as property binding.

We can respond to any native DOM event by surrounding it with parentheses and assign it to a method on the component class. Let's see how we can respond to the click event on our button. We need to wrap the click event of the button in parentheses, and assign a method that will be invoked in return:

```
@Component({
  selector: 'app-root',
  template: `
    <button (click)="clickHandler()">
      click me!</button>
    `
})
export class AppComponent {
  clickHandler() {
    console.log('button clicked!');
  }
}
```

Let's use data binding techniques to create a simple toggle component:

```
@Component({
  selector: 'app-root',
  template: `
    <h2 (click)="toggeld = !toggeld ">Click me to toggle some content1</h2>
    <p *ngIf="toggeld">Toggeld content</p>
    `
})
export class AppComponent {}
```

Two-way bindings

We learned how to use one way data bindings using properties and events. Angular introduces a third option to use with input controls. This directive is called `ngModel`. The syntax can be a little strange, because this directive combines property and event bindings together.

With `ngModel`, we can easily achieve two-way data binding easily. In the following example, we will bind username and password inputs to a user object:

```
@Component({
  selector: 'app-root',
  template: `
    <input type="text"  [(ngModel)]="user.username">
    <input type="password"  [(ngModel)]="user.password">

    <button (click)="sendUser()">Send</button>
  `
})
export class AppComponent {
  private user = {
    username: '',
    password: ''
  }

  sendUser(){
    console.log(this.user);
  }
}
```

Summary

Throughout this chapter, we transform our static component to a dynamic component using core directives and data binding.

Angular 2 keeps the data binding easy, much like Angular 1. The ability to bind data to native DOM properties and events directly is a powerful feature. The core directives of Angular 2 includes only a few directives that give us some extra functionality that otherwise is hard to achieve.

Component Communication

6

Up until now, we have built a single component, but the real power of Angular components is building the interaction between them. in this chapter, we will learn how components can communicate in different ways:

- Pass data from the parent component to the child through properties
- Define custom events on a child component for the parent to listen to
- Communicate via local variables
- Query child components using the parent component

Passing data via properties

The parent component can pass data to the child component through properties. There are two ways that define input properties for a component:

- By creating an input array on the component decorator
- By using the @Input decorator for decorating a class property

Using the component input array is simple and straightforward. Just declare an input array and populate it with strings that represent the name of the property you are expecting:

```
[app.component.ts]
import { Component } from '@angular/core';

@Component({
  selector: 'child-component',
  inputs:    ['title'],
  template: `<h2>{{ title }}</h2>`
})
```

```
export class ChildComponent {}

@Component({
  selector: 'app-root',
  template: `
    <h1>Component Interactions</h1>
    <child-component [title]="title" ></child-component>
  `
})
export class AppComponent {
  private title: string = "Sub title for child";
}
```

In this example, we created a child component, which defined an input array with a single string named `title` that represents a property that the parent component can bind to and pass data through.

Don't forget to add the `ChildComponent` class to the declarations attribute of the `AppModule`. Otherwise, this component can't be used within the template of the `AppComponent`. This configuration is required each time you need to use a component or a directive in another one and within the same module:

```
[app.module.ts]
import { BrowserModule } from '@angular/platform-browser';
import { NgModule } from '@angular/core';
import { FormsModule } from '@angular/forms';
import { HttpModule } from '@angular/http';
import { AppComponent, ChildComponent } from './app.component';

@NgModule({
  declarations: [
    AppComponent,
    ChildComponent
  ],
  imports: [
    BrowserModule
  ],
  providers: [],
  bootstrap: [AppComponent]
})
export class AppModule { }
```

The approach of the input array is suitable when we don't need to access the input in the `Component` class, and we don't care about the type of the input.

Alternatively, we can bind an input to a class property using the `@Input()` decorator:

```
[app.component.ts]
import { Component, Input } from '@angular/core';

@Component({
  selector: 'child-component',
  template: `<h2>{{ title }}</h2>`
})
export class ChildComponent {
  @Input() private title: string;
}

@Component({
  selector: 'app-root',
  template: `
    <h1>Component Interactions</h1>
    <child-component [title]="title"></child-component>
  `
})
export class AppComponent {
  private title: string = 'Sub title for child';
}
```

Binding to a class property (the second example) is considered to be a best practice when dealing with inputs.

An input can be a primitive or an object.

Emitting custom events

When the child component needs to communicate with its parent component, it can emit an event. This technique keeps the child component de-coupled from its parent (de-coupled: doesn't need to know its parents).

In Angular, we need to use a class named `EventEmitter` if we want to emit events.

You need to instantiate the `EventEmitter` class, assign it to a class property, and call the `emit` method.

In the following example, the child component will emit a custom event named `TitleClicked` when the user clicks on the title:

```
[app.component.ts]
import { Component, Input, EventEmitter, Output } from '@angular/
core';

@Component({
  selector: 'child-component',
  template: `<h2 (click)="titleClicked.emit()">{{ title }}</h2>`
})
export class ChildComponent {
  @Input() private title: string;
  @Output() private titleClicked = new EventEmitter<any>();
}

@Component({
  selector: 'app-root',
  template: `
    <h1>Component Interactions</h1>
    <child-component [title]="title"
    (titleClicked)="clickHandler()"></child-component>
  `
})
export class AppComponent {
  private title: string = 'Sub title for child';
  clickHandler() {
    console.log('Clicked!');
  }
}
```

First, we imported the `EventEmitter` class and the `Output` decorator from Angular core. Then, we created a class property named `titleClicked` and assigned it to a fresh instance of the `EventEmitter` class.

Then, we bound the native click event of the `<h2>` element and called the `emit()` method of the `titleClicked` object.

The parent component can now bind to this event.

Referencing with a local variable

One component can access another component's properties and methods using local variables. In the following example, we create a local variable for the child component that becomes accessible within the template:

```
[app.component.ts]
import { Component } from '@angular/core';

@Component({
  selector: 'child-component',
  template: `
    <h2>Content Header</h2>
    <p *ngIf="flag">Toggleable Content</p>
  `
})
export class ChildComponent {
  private flag: boolean = false;
  toggle() {
    this.flag = !this.flag;
  }
}

@Component({
  selector : 'app-root',
  template : `
    <h1>Component Interactions</h1>
    <button (click)="child.toggle()">Toggle Child</button>
    <child-component #child></child-component>
  `
})
export class AppComponent {}
```

We create a local variable using the # symbol.

The method in the child component must be public, otherwise Angular will throw an exception.

This technique is very useful in some cases because it doesn't require any code inside the component class. On the other hand, the reference context is just inside the template.

If you need to access the child component inside the parent component, you need to inject a reference to the child component using the `@ViewChild` decorator.

Consider the following example:

```
[app.component.ts]
import { Component, ViewChild } from '@angular/core';

@Component({
  selector: 'child-component',
  template: `
    <h2>Content Header</h2>
    <p *ngIf="flag">Toggleable Content</p>
  `
})
export class ChildComponent {
  private flag: boolean = false;
  toggle(){
    this.flag = !this.flag;
  }
}

@Component({
  selector: 'app-root',
  template: `
    <h1>Component Interactions</h1>
    <button (click)="toggle()">Toggle Child</button>
    <child-component></child-component>
  `
})
export class AppComponent {
  @ViewChild(ChildComponent)
  private childComponent: ChildComponent;
  toggle(){
    this.childComponent.toggle();
  }
}
```

The parent component is using the `@ViewChild` decorator (imported from angular core) passing the name of the component, and assigning it to a local class member named `childComponent`.

If we have more than one instance of the child component, we can use the `@ViewChildren` decorator instead.

Querying child components with the parent component

The `@ViewChildren` component will provide a reference to all of the children components of a given type as a `QueryList`, which contains an array of child instances.

Consider the following example:

```
[app.component.ts]
import { Component, ViewChildren, QueryList } from '@angular/core';

@Component({
  selector: 'child-component',
  template: `
    <h2>Content Header</h2>
    <p *ngIf="flag">Toggleable Content</p>
  `
})
export class ChildComponent {
  private flag: boolean = false;

  toggle(){
    this.flag = !this.flag;
  }
}

@Component({
  selector: 'app-root',
  template: `
    <h1>Component Interactions</h1>
    <button (click)="toggle()">Toggle Child</button>
    <child-component></child-component>
    <child-component></child-component>
    <child-component></child-component>
  `
```

```
})
export class AppComponent {
  @ViewChildren(ChildComponent)
  private children: QueryList<ChildComponent>;
  toggle(){
    this.children.forEach(child => child.toggle())
  }
}
```

Both `ViewChildren` and the `QueryList` are imported from Angular core.

Summary

Components can interact and communicate in many ways. Each technique is suitable for a certain situation. The main difference is related to the scope of communication: template context or component class context.

This flexibility enables us to create complex component compositions that easily share data and interactions, which consists of APIs.

In the next chapter, we will build useful components and also learn about Angular 2 change detection and the component life cycle.

7
Putting It All Together

It's time to take everything we have learned about components and put it into practice. In this chapter, we will build useful components. We will also learn about Angular 2 change detection and the component life cycle.

The following are the topics that we will cover:

- Resetting the development environment
- Building a simple accordion component
- Extending the accordion component tree
- Extending hooking to the component life cycle events

Preparing our development environment

It's time to create a new project with `angular-cli` as described in *Chapter 2, Setting Up an Angular 2 Development Environment with angular-cli*. We will create a new directory called `components` to contain all the components we will implement in this chapter.

We will later create two other subdirectories in this chapter, `accordion` and `user-info`, when implementing the corresponding components:

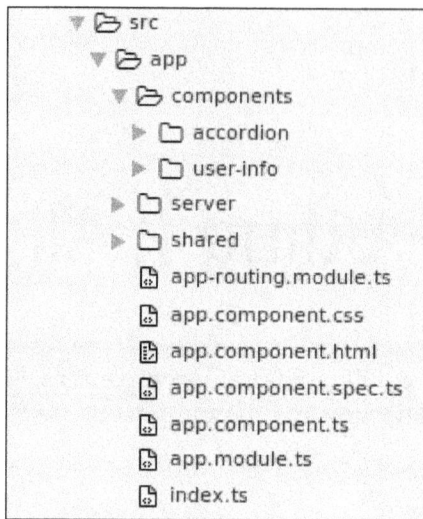

```
▼ 🗁 src
  ▼ 🗁 app
    ▼ 🗁 components
      ▶ 🗀 accordion
      ▶ 🗀 user-info
    ▶ 🗀 server
    ▶ 🗀 shared
      📄 app-routing.module.ts
      📄 app.component.css
      📄 app.component.html
      📄 app.component.spec.ts
      📄 app.component.ts
      📄 app.module.ts
      📄 index.ts
```

The last thing before starting to build our new components is to clean up our root component. Open `index.ts` and clean it as follows:

```
[app.component.ts]
import { Component } from '@angular/core';

@Component({
  selector: 'app-root',
  template: '<h1>Angular2 Components</h1>'
})
export class AppComponent {}
```

Open your browser and make sure that the component has rendered without any errors:

← → C 🗋 localhost:4200

Angular2 Components

Now we are ready to start developing our new components.

The accordion component

The first component that we are going to build will be an `accordion` component. The accordion is composed from two components: the accordion wrapper and an accordion tab. Let's start implementing the `accordion` tab first.

Inside the components directory, create a new directory called `accordion`. Inside it, create the `accordion-tab.ts` file, and paste the following code:

```
[accordion-tab.ts]
import { Component } from '@angular/core';

@Component({
  selector: 'accordion-tab',
  styles: [`
    .accordion-tab {
      width: 500px;
      border: 1px solid black;
      border-collapse: collapse;
    }
    .accordion-heading {
      padding: 5px;
      background-color: lightblue;
      cursor: pointer;
    }
  `],
  template: `
    <div class="accordion-tab">
      <div class="accordion-heading">Accordion Title</div>
      <div>
        <ng-content></ng-content>
      </div>
    </div>
  `
})
export class AccordionTab {}
```

The component decorator is straightforward. We throw some CSS and a template that includes a `<ng-content>` tag to use an insertion point for the accordion tab content.

To test it, let's render the `accordion-tab` file. Open `app.component.ts` and update the code:

```
[app.component.ts]
import { Component } from '@angular/core';
import { AccordionTab } from './components/accordion/accordion-tab';

@Component({
  selector: 'app-root',
  template:`
    <div>
      <accordion-tab>Accordion Content</accordion-tab>
      <accordion-tab></accordion-tab>
      <accordion-tab></accordion-tab>
    </div>
  `
})
export class AppComponent {}
```

Don't forget to add the `AccordionTab` class to the declarations attribute of the root module. This operation will be required for all custom components implemented in this chapter. Open the `app.module.ts` file and update it as follows:

```
[app.module.ts]
import { BrowserModule } from '@angular/platform-browser';
import { NgModule } from '@angular/core';
import { FormsModule } from '@angular/forms';
import { HttpModule } from '@angular/http';
import { AppComponent } from './app.component';
import { AccordionTab } from './components/accordion/accordion-tab';

@NgModule({
  declarations: [
    AppComponent,
    AccordionTab
  ],
  imports: [
    BrowserModule,
    FormsModule,
    HttpModule
  ],
  providers: [],
  bootstrap: [AppComponent]
})
export class AppModule { }
```

Now, let's open the browser to make sure that the component is rendered as expected:

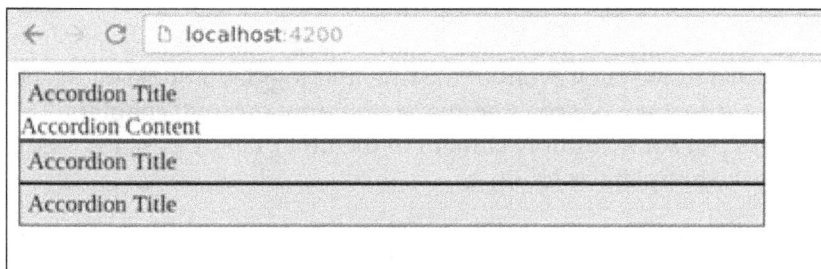

Next, let's implement the toggle action of `accordion-tab`. Open `accordion-tab.ts` and update the template and the Component class:

```
[accordion-tab.ts]
import { Component } from '@angular/core';

@Component({
  selector: 'accordion-tab',
  styles: [`
    .accordion-tab {
      width: 500px;
      border: 1px solid black;
      border-collapse: collapse;
    }
    .accordion-heading {
      padding: 5px;
      background-color: lightblue;
      cursor: pointer;
    }
  `],
  template: `
    <div class="accordion-tab">
      <div class="accordion-heading"
        (click)="toggleContent()">Accordion Title</div>
      <div class="accordion-body">
        <ng-content *ngIf="extended"></ng-content>
      </div>
    </div>
  `
})
export class AccordionTab {
  extended: boolean = false;
```

```
    toggleContent() {
      this.extended = !this.extended
    }
  }
```

We bind a method to the click event of the title that toggles a Boolean, which trigger the ngIf directive. We covered that in the previous two chapters. To test our component, let's put some dummy content in the other tabs. Open app.component. ts and update the template as follows:

```
[app.component.ts]
import { Component } from '@angular/core';
import { AccordionTab } from './accordion/accordion-tab.ts';

@Component({
  selector: 'app-root',
  template:`
    <div>
      <accordion-tab>Accordion Content</accordion-tab>
      <accordion-tab>Accordion Content</accordion-tab>
      <accordion-tab>Accordion Content</accordion-tab>
    </div>
    `
})
export class AppComponent {}
```

Now, we can open the browser and test our component. When we click on a tab title, the corresponding content is toggled. But the tabs should work together. Only one tab can be extended. To achieve this, we can wrap the accordion-tab component with a component that implements this logic.

Before we do it, we need to make sure that each of the objects in the users array that we get from the server (users.json in our case) has a unique id. Open users.json and make sure it is similar to the following:

```
[users.json]
[
  {
    "id": 1,
    "name": "Jhon Darn",
    "email": "jhon@email.com",
    "birthday": "5/6/1979",
    "gender": "male",
    "status": "active",
    "role": "employee",
    "phoneNumbers": [
```

```
        "+972-123-9873",
        "+972-352-8922",
        "+972-667-2973"
    ]
  },
  (...)
```

Now, create a new file called `accordion.ts` inside the `accordion` folder and let's lay down the basic implementation:

```
[accordion.ts]
import { Component } from '@angular/core';
import { Http } from '@angular/http';
import 'rxjs/add/operator/map';
import { AccordionTab } from './accordion-tab';

@Component({
  selector: 'accordion',
  template: `
    <div>
      <accordion-tab *ngFor="let user of users"
                  (click)="toggle(user)"
                  [extended]="isActive(user)"
                  [title]="user.name">
                <pre>{{ user | json }}</pre>
      </accordion-tab>
    </div>
  `
})
export class Accordion {  users;
  activeUserId = 0;

  constructor(http: Http) {
    http.get('/app/server/users.json')
        .map(result => result.json())
        .subscribe(result => this.users = result);
  }

  isActive(user) {
    return user.id === this.activeUserId;
  }

  toggle(user) {
    this.isActive(user) ?
        this.activeUserId = 0 : this.activeUserId = user.id;
  }
}
```

We used the HTTP service to pull the user's data from a static JSON, and we iterate over the `users` array — repeating the accordion-tab component. On each `accordion-tab` component, we bind a method to a click event and bind dynamic data to the properties. We are also using the `json` pipe fill some content inside the accordion tabs.

The logic for selecting an active tab is very easy to implement inside the `Component` class.

Next, we need to refactor the `accordion-tab` and define its input and output interface:

```typescript
[accordion-tab.ts]
import {
    Component, Input, Output
} from '@angular/core';

@Component({
  selector: 'accordion-tab',
  styles: [`
    .accordion-tab {
      width: 500px;
      border: 1px solid black;
      border-collapse: collapse;
    }
    .accordion-heading {
      padding: 5px;
      background-color: lightblue;
      cursor: pointer;
    }
  `],
  template:`
    <div class="accordion-tab">
      <div class="accordion-heading"
        (click)="toggleContent()">{{title}}</div>
      <div class="accordion-body">
        <content *ngIf="extended"></content>
      </div>
    </div>
  `
})
export class AccordionTab {
  @Input() extended;
  @Input() title;
```

```
    toggleContent() {
      this.extended = !this.extended
    }
  }
```

The simple accordion is now ready. We used almost everything we have learned to craft this widget. Note that we didn't have to write a lot of code. Angular's built-in directives and binding system did all the heavy lifting for us. To test it in the browser, open `app.component.ts` and render the `<accordion>` component:

```
[app.component.ts]
import { Component } from '@angular/core';
import { Accordion } from './components/accordion/accordion';

@Component({
  selector: 'app-root',
  template: `<accordion></accordion>`
})
export class AppComponent {}
```

Open the browser and check the result. Each time we click on an accordion tab, it is the only one that gets extended:

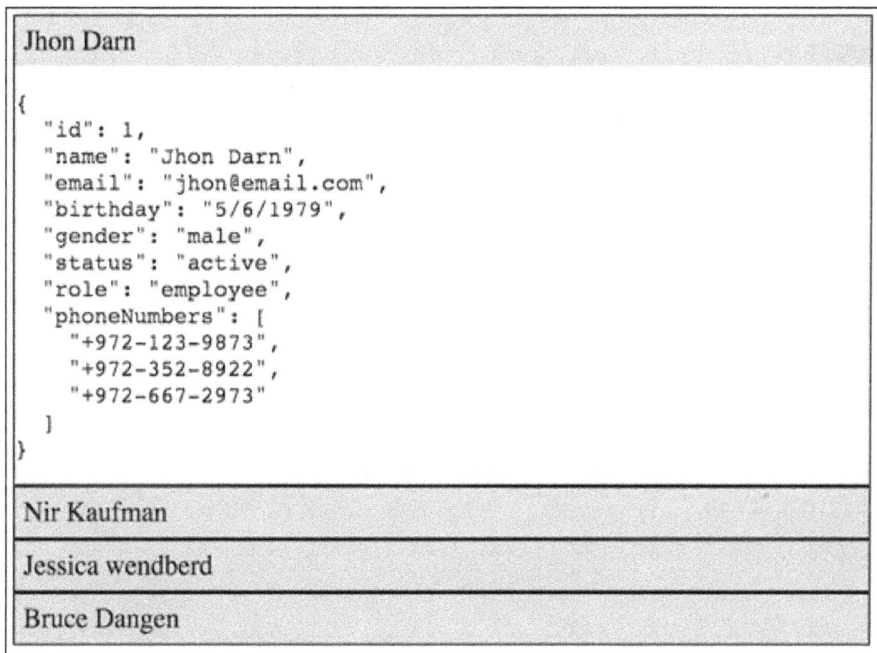

```
Jhon Darn

{
  "id": 1,
  "name": "Jhon Darn",
  "email": "jhon@email.com",
  "birthday": "5/6/1979",
  "gender": "male",
  "status": "active",
  "role": "employee",
  "phoneNumbers": [
    "+972-123-9873",
    "+972-352-8922",
    "+972-667-2973"
  ]
}

Nir Kaufman

Jessica wendberd

Bruce Dangen
```

Before we move forward, let's make the accordion extended only when clicking its
title, and the whole tab. For this, we will emit a custom event when clicking on the
title and then bind to this event from the parent component, which is the accordion:

```typescript
[accordion-tab.ts]
import {
    Component, Input, Output, EventEmitter
} from '@angular/core';

@Component({
  selector: 'accordion-tab',
  styles: [`
    .accordion-tab {
      width: 500px;
      border: 1px solid black;
      border-collapse: collapse;
    }
    .accordion-heading {
      padding: 5px;
      background-color: lightblue;
      cursor: pointer;
    }
  `],
  template: `
    <div class="accordion-tab">
     <div class="accordion-heading"
          (click)="toggleContent()">{{title}}</div>
     <div>
      <ng-content *ngIf="extended"></ng-content>
     </div>
    </div>
  `
})
export class AccordionTab {
  @Input() extended : boolean;
  @Input() title : string;
  @Output() toggle = new EventEmitter<any>();
  toggleContent() {
    this.toggle.emit(null)
  }
}
```

That's it for the `accordion-tab` component. Let's move to the `accordion` component and bind to this event:

```
[accordion.ts]
import { Component, Inject } from '@angular/core';
import { Http } from '@angular/http';
import 'rxjs/add/operator/map';
import { AccordionTab } from './accordion-tab';
@Component({
  selector: 'accordion',
  template: `
    <div>
      <accordion-tab *ngFor="let user of users"
                     (toggle)="toggle(user)"
                     [extended]="isActive(user)"
                     [title]="user.name">
        <pre>{{ user | json }}</pre>
      </accordion-tab>
    </div>
  `
})
export class Accordion {
  users;
  activeUserId = 0;

  constructor(http: Http) {
    http.get('/app/server/users.json')
        .map(result => result.json())
        .subscribe(result => this.users = result);
  }
  isActive(user) {
    return user.id === this.activeUserId;
  }
  toggle(user) {
    this.isActive(user) ?
        this.activeUserId = 0 : this.activeUserId = user.id;
  }
}
```

Now we can render the accordion component and see the results.
In `app.component.ts'` include the following:

```
[app.component.ts]
import { Component } from '@angular/core';
import { Accordion } from './components/accordion/accordion';

@Component({
  selector: 'app-root',
  template:`<accordion></accordion>`
})
export class AppComponent {}
```

Open the browser and check the results. The accordion works as expected.

Extending the accordion component tree

Let's add another component to our accordion tree. Instead of rendering raw JSON as a tab content, let's reuse the user information component that we built on in *Chapter 4*, *Building a Basic Component*, and *Chapter 5*, *Building Dynamic Components*. For this, just create a `user-info` subdirectory in the `components` directory and copy the corresponding TypeScript files into this directory. The only file we need to refactor is `accordion.ts`:

```
[accordion.ts]
import { Component, Inject, ViewEncapsulation } from '@angular/core';
import { Http } from '@angular/http';
import 'rxjs/add/operator/map';
import { AccordionTab } from './accordion-tab';
import { UserInformation } from '../user-info/user-info';

@Component({
  selector: 'accordion',
  template: `
    <div>
      <accordion-tab *ngFor="let user of users"
                     (toggle)="toggle(user)"
                     [extended]="isActive(user)"
                     [title]="user.name">
        <user-info [user]="user"></user-info>
      </accordion-tab>
    </div>
```

```
})
export class Accordion {
  users;
  activeUserId = 0;
  constructor(http: Http) {
    http.get('app/server/users.json')
        .map(result => result.json())
        .subscribe(result => this.users = result);
  }
  isActive(user) {
    return user.id === this.activeUserId;
  }
  toggle(user) {
    this.isActive(user) ?
        this.activeUserId = 0 : this.activeUserId = user.id;
  }
}
```

All we needed to do is to import the user info component, declare it in the component metadata, and use it in our template, binding the `user` variable to the `User` property that the component expects.

The component life cycle

Component instances have a life cycle that we can hook into. Currently, our mini application contains four components: `App`, `accordion`, `accordion-tab`, and `user-info`, but a typical Angular application will contain tens of component trees that Angular will create, update, and destroy during our application's lifetime.

For demo purposes, we will simulate a server call that returns other data. For this, create a file called `other-users.json` inside the `server` directory and paste this code into it:

```
[other-users.json]
[
  {
    "id": 5,
    "name": "Michael jackson",
    "email": "jackson@email.com",
    "birthday": "22/3/1974",
    "gender": "male",
    "status": "onhold",
    "role": "manager",
```

```
    "phoneNumbers": [
      "+972-123-9873"
    ]
  },
  (...)
]
```

On the accordion component template, we will add a button that will fetch this new data and implement the `fetchData` method on the `Component` class:

```
[accordion.ts]
import { Component, Inject } from '@angular/core';
import { Http } from '@angular/http';
import 'rxjs/add/operator/map';
import { AccordionTab } from './accordion-tab';
import { UserInformation } from '../user-info/user-info';

@Component({
  selector: 'accordion',
  template: `
    <div>
      <button (click)="fetchData('other-users.json')">update data</
button>
      <accordion-tab *ngFor="let user of users"
                     (toggle)="toggle(user)"
                     [extended]="isActive(user)"
                     [title]="user.name">
        <user-info [user]="user"></user-info>
      </accordion-tab>
    </div>
  `
})
export class Accordion {
  users;
  activeUserId = 0;

  constructor(private http: Http) {
    this.fetchData('users.json');
  }
  isActive(user) {
    return user.id === this.activeUserId;
  }

  fetchData(subPath) {
    this.http.get(`/app/server/${subPath}`)
```

```
        .map(result => result.json())
        .subscribe(result => this.users = result);
}

toggle(user) {
    this.isActive(user) ?
        this.activeUserId = 0 : this.activeUserId = user.id;
}
}
```

Now, each time we click on the button, the user's data is updated and the accordion re-rendered. Open the browser, click on the button, and watch the accordion data change.

Life cycle event interfaces

In order to run our own logic on each one of the component life cycle events, we need to implement the desired method that corresponds to the event we want to react to. Each one of those events is published as a TypeScript interface, which we can implement in our component class. The use of TypeScript interfaces is optional and won't affect our application in any way at all. You can learn about TypeScript interfaces from the documentation on the TypeScript website at http://www. typescriptlang.org/docs/handbook/interfaces.html. We won't use this in our code examples.

OnInit and OnDestroy

The simplest, most straightforward, and most easy-to-understand life cycle event hooks are onInit and onDestroy.

The ngOnInit method is called after the component data-bound properties have been checked for the first time, and ngOnDestroy will be called right before the component instance is destroyed by Angular. In our component hierarchy, we will implement both of these methods on the user-info class:

```
[user-info.ts]
import {
  Component, Input,
  OnInit, OnDestroy
} from '@angular/core';

@Component({
```

```
    selector: 'user-info',
    styleUrls: ['./user-info.css'],
    templateUrl: './user-info.html'
})
export class UserInformation implements OnInit, OnDestroy {
    @Input()
    user;

    fontSize = '20px';
    editMode = false;
    randomNumber;

    ngOnInit(){
        console.log('UserInformation initialized');
    }

    ngOnDestroy(){
        console.log('UserInformation Destroy');
    }

    toggleEditMode() {
        this.editMode = !this.editMode;
    }

    onSubmit(data) {
        Object.assign(this.user, data);
        this.editMode = false;
    }
}
```

Now, open the browser and make sure the console is visible. You should see four logs that indicate that each of the user components have been initialized:

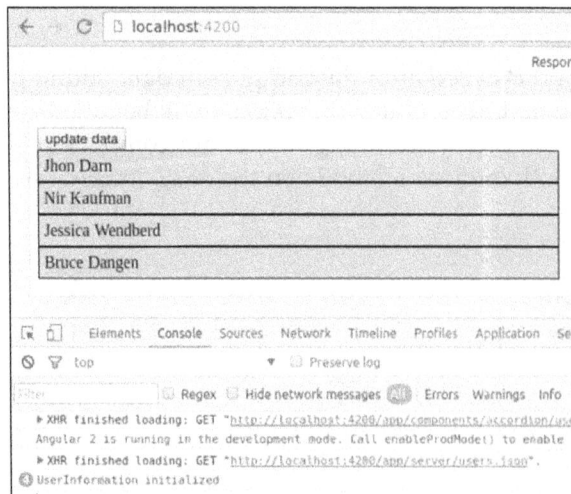

Now, click on the button to pull new data from the server. You should see four logs for each user information component that have been destroyed, and three logs for the new components that are created for the new data:

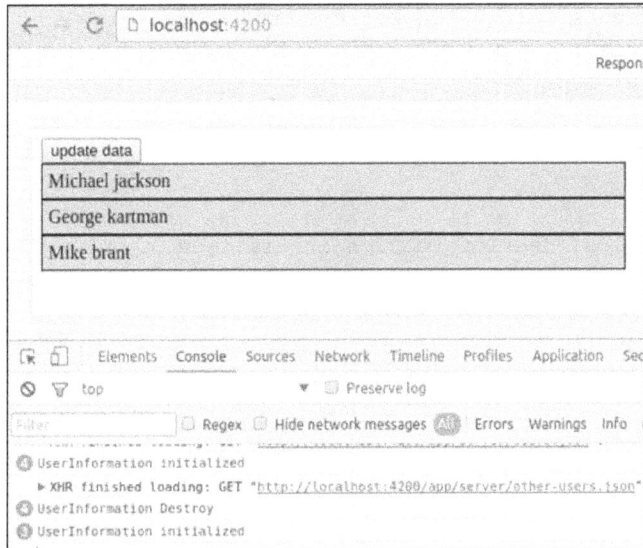

The OnInit method is a good place to run code after the components have been initialized (data bounded properties have been resolved), and before one of the child components has been initialized. OnDestroy is a good place for cleanup or persistence code for the component's state just before it is ripped from the DOM.

OnChanges

OnChanges has a method named ngOnChanges that will be called after all the data-binding properties have been checked. Angular passes a change object that contains a key named after the property that changed, and an instance of a SimpleChange object. The SimpleChange object contains the previous value and the current value. Let's implement this method in our user-info component:

```
[user-info.ts]
import {
  Component, Input,
  OnInit, OnDestroy, OnChanges
} from '@angular/core';

@Component({
  selector: 'user-info',
```

```
    styleUrls: ['./user-info.css'],
    templateUrl: './user-info.html'
})
export class UserInformation
        implements OnInit, OnDestroy, OnChanges {
    @Input() user;
    fontSize = '20px';
    editMode = false;
    randomNumber;

    ngOnInit(){
      console.log('UserInformation initialized');
    }

    ngOnDestroy(){
      console.log('UserInformation Destroy');
    }

    ngOnChanges(changes){
      console.log('onChanges', changes);
    }

    toggleEditMode() {
      this.editMode = !this.editMode;
    }

    onSubmit(data) {
      Object.assign(this.user, data);
      this.editMode = false;
    }
}
```

In the browser console, we will see four logs:

```
onChanges ▼ Object {user: SimpleChange}
              ▼ user: SimpleChange
                 ▶ currentValue: Object
                 ▶ previousValue: Object
                 ▶ __proto__: SimpleChange
              ▶ __proto__: Object
onChanges ▶ Object {user: SimpleChange}
onChanges ▶ Object {user: SimpleChange}
onChanges ▶ Object {user: SimpleChange}
```

If you are familiar with Angular 1.x, you can think of the `OnChange` method as a `$scope.$watch` function. It will be called any time the data changes, and contains both the new and the old values.

Other life cycle events

Besides the `init`, `changes`, and `destroy` events, we can hook four more component life cycle events:

- `AfterContentInit`: This is called after the component's content is fully initialized
- `AfterContentChecked`: This is called after each time the component is checked
- `AfterViewInit`: This is called after the component's view has initialized
- `AfterViewChecked`: This is called after the component's view has been checked

Each of them can be implemented in the same way as the previous examples.

Summary

Through this chapter, we took everything we have learned so far about components and built a useful accordion widget that is composed of four components. An Angular 2 application is a collection of dynamic components that communicate with each other using properties as an input, and events as output. We can hook into each important life cycle of a component, for example, when a component is initialized or destroyed, and run our own logic.

8

Integrating Third-Party Components

There are a lot of UI components built with other libraries that we might want to use in our Angular 2 application. Throughout this chapter we will integrate a tooltip widget from the popular bootstrap library.

Importing the bootstrap and jQuery libraries are the topics that we cover in this chapter.

Preparing our development environment

Before we continue, let's create a new project. Open `app.component.ts` and remove the external links to the HTML template and the CSS file:

```
[app.component.ts]
import { Component } from '@angular/core';

@Component({
  selector: 'app-root',
  template: `<h1>Angular2 components</h1>`
})
export class AppComponent {}
```

Importing dependencies

Since we are going to wrap a component from the bootstrap library, we first need to download and import the bootstrap library and its dependencies and import it in to our code. The first step will be to install `bootstrap` with `npm`. Open the Terminal, make sure that you are inside the project root, and type `npm install bootstrap -S`. This command will download the bootstrap files into the `node_modules` and write it on the `package.json`.

Since bootstrap is dependent on jQuery library, we need to install it as well. We will use npm for it as well. In the Terminal, type npm install jquery -S.

We also need to install corresponding typings for these two libraries to be able to compile the application. The names of the corresponding typing modules are the same as the target libraries but with the @types prefix. To install them, just use the following command:

npm install @types/jquery @types/bootstrap --save-dev

The CSS file of the Bootstrap library needs to be configured globally for the application in the styles section of the angular-cli.json file:

```
[angular-cli.json]
{
  "project": {
    "version": "1.0.0-beta.16",
    "name": "ng-components"
  },
  "apps": [
    {
      "root": "src",
      "outDir": "dist",
      "assets": "assets",
      "index": "index.html",
      "main": "main.ts",
      "test": "test.ts",
      "tsconfig": "tsconfig.json",
      "prefix": "app",
      "mobile": false,
      "styles": [
        "styles.css",
        "../node_modules/bootstrap/dist/css/bootstrap.css"
      ],
      "scripts": [
      ],
      "environments": {
        "source": "environments/environment.ts",
        "dev": "environments/environment.ts",
        "prod": "environments/environment.prod.ts"
      }
    }
  ],
  (...)
}
```

Since the latest versions of the Angular CLI rely on Webpack, we use its expose loader to make available jQuery globally to the Bootstrap library. The latter needs this to extend jQuery by adding a set of methods such as tooltip and collapse. To install the expose loader, just use the following command:

```
npm install expose-loader --save-dev
```

We can now import both jQuery and Bootstrap where we need them using the import clause.

Before we move forward, open app.component.ts and add the following import statements for the jQuery and Bootstrap libraries:

```
[app.component.ts]
import { Component } from '@angular/core';
import 'expose?jQuery!jquery';
import 'bootstrap';
import * as $ from 'jquery';

@Component({
  selector: 'app-root',
  template: `<h1>Angular2 components</h1>`
})
export class AppComponent {}
```

Bootstrap tooltip component

Angular 2's ability to bind to element properties and events without the need for custom directives enables us to integrate with third-party code easily. Bootstrap uses some custom attributes to make the tooltip work. We can use it as is. Open app.component.ts and add the bootstrap attributes to the heading to display a tooltip from the bottom. We also need to leverage the AfterViewInit hook to initialize the tooltip when the template is rendered:

```
[app.component.ts]
import { Component, AfterViewInit } from '@angular/core';
import 'expose?jQuery!jquery';
import 'bootstrap';
import * as $ from 'jquery';

@Component({
  selector: 'app-root',
  template: `
    <h1 data-toggle="tooltip"
        data-placement="bottom"
```

```
        title="A Tooltip on the right">Angular2 components</h1>

})
export class AppComponent implements AfterViewInit {
  ngAfterViewInit() {
    $('h1').tooltip();
  }
}
```

Now, let's open the browser and test it. Hover over the title and wait for the tooltip to appear at the bottom:

Now, let's integrate it with Angular and make it dynamic. The process is straightforward. We can bind to each property that we want to control. Let's start with the title.

Open `app.component.ts` and add the following code:

```
[app.component.ts]
import { Component, AfterViewInit } from '@angular/core';
import 'expose?jQuery!jquery';
import 'bootstrap';
import * as $ from 'jquery';

@Component({
  selector: 'app-root',
  template: `
    <input type="text" [(ngModel)]="title" placeholder="enter custom
title..">
    <h1 data-toggle="tooltip"
        data-placement="bottom"
        [title]="title">Angular2 components</h1>
```

```
})
export class AppComponent implements AfterViewInit {
  ngAfterViewInit() {
    $('h1').tooltip();
  }
}
```

We didn't have to write a single line of code in our component class to make it work. Open the browser, type a title, and hover over the title to see the result:

Bootstrap collapse component

Let's try another example, but this time we will bind to events as well. For this example we will use another widget from the bootstrap library called `collapse`. In the `components` folder, create a new folder named `collapse`. Inside it, create a file named `collapse.ts` for our component and a file named `collapse.html` for the component template.

Open `collapse.ts` and paste the following code. This is an example collapse widget that was taken *as-is* from the bootstrap website (http://getbootstrap.com/javascript/#collapse):

```
[collapse.ts]
import { Component, AfterViewInit } from '@angular/core';
import * as $ from 'jquery';

@Component({
  selector: 'collapse',
  templateUrl: './collapse.html'
})
```

```
export class Collapse implements AfterViewInit {
  ngAfterViewInit() {
    $('.collapse').collapse();
  }
}
```

Open `collapse.html` and paste in the following:

```
[collapse.html]
<button class="btn btn-primary"
        data-toggle="collapse"
        data-target="#collapseExample"
        aria-expanded="false"
        aria-controls="collapseExample">
  Collapse!
</button>

<div class="collapse"
     id="collapseExample">
  <div class="well">
    Integrating third party is easy with angular2!
  </div>
</div>
```

Let's render the component. Open `app.component.ts`, import the `collapse` component, and use it in the template as follows:

```
[app.component.ts]
import { Component } from '@angular/core';
import 'expose?jQuery!jquery';
import 'bootstrap';

@Component({
  selector: 'app-root',
  template: '<collapse></collapse>'
})
export class AppComponent {}
```

Don't forget to add the `Collapse` class to the `declarations` attribute of the root module of the application to make the `collapse` component usable, as shown in the following code:

```
[app.module.ts]
import { BrowserModule } from '@angular/platform-browser';
import { NgModule } from '@angular/core';
import { FormsModule } from '@angular/forms';
import { HttpModule } from '@angular/http';
import { AppComponent } from './app.component';
import { Collapse } from './components/collapse/collapse';

@NgModule({
  declarations: [
    AppComponent,
    Collapse
  ],
  imports: [
    BrowserModule,
    FormsModule,
    HttpModule
  ],
  providers: [],
  bootstrap: [AppComponent]
})
export class AppModule { }
```

Now, open the browser to test the collapse event:

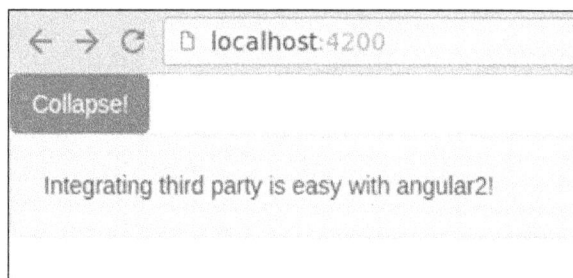

We already know how to bind to properties from the tooltip example. In this example, we will bind to the collapse events.

According to the bootstrap documents, the collapse fires four events throughout it's life cycle. We will focus on two of them:

- `show.bs.collapse`: This method fires when the `show` method is called.

- `hide.bs.collapse`: This method fires when the `hide` method is called.

If we want to listen to those events, we need to hold a reference to the DOM element. For this, we will inject `ElementRef`. Open `collapse.ts` and the following code:

```
[collapse.ts]
import { Component, Inject, ElementRef } from '@angular/core';
import * as $ from 'jquery';

@Component({
  selector: 'collapse',
  templateUrl: './collapse.html'
})
export class Collapse {
  constructor(element: ElementRef) {
    $(element.nativeElement)
      .on('show.bs.collapse',
      ()=> console.log('handle show event'));
    $(element.nativeElement)
      .on('hide.bs.collapse',
      ()=> console.log('handle hideevent'));
  }
}
```

There is a lot of ways to listen to an event on an element. We choose to use jQuery to wrap the native element and register an event listener for the collapse.

You can open the browser and watch the logs in the console corresponding to the collapse events:

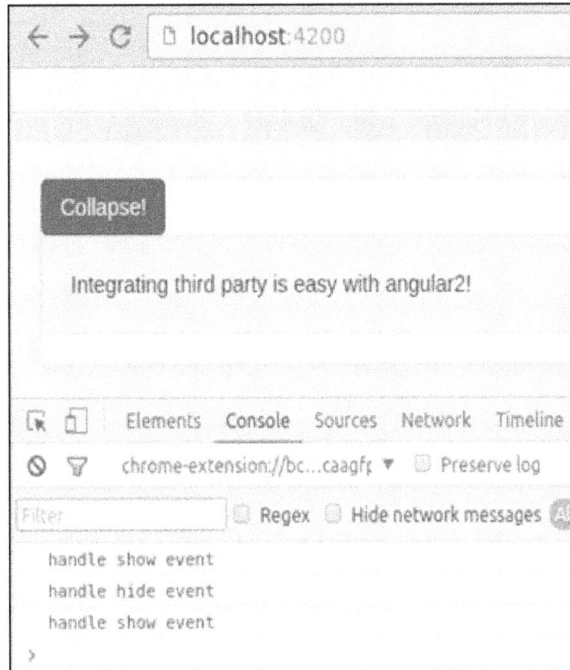

Summary

Angular 2 plays well with third-party code by enabling binding to native properties naturally. On the other hand, if we need to hold a reference to the DOM element, we can inject `ElementRef` in to our component.

9
Angular 2 Directives

Throughout this book, we learned how to craft Angular 2 components. Before we end our journey, it's important to understand that Angular 2 didn't kill the concept of directives. As a matter of fact, a component *is* a directive. In this chapter, we will introduce Angular 2 directives and how to use them.

The following are the topics that we will cover:

- The difference between components and directives in Angular 2
- Angular 2 directive types
- How to build a simple attribute directive
- How to build a simple structural directive

Components and directives in Angular 2

Up until now, we have built components. But components do not replace the directives that we are familiar with from Angular 1. If you are not familiar with Angular 1 directives, don't worry, we will explain the difference in a minute.

Let's start by defining what a directive is in Angular terminology: a directive is a custom attribute or an element that extends HTML tags by adding custom behavior.

In Angular 2, we have three types of directive: component directive, attribute directive, and structural directive. We are already familiar with components, so let's define the other types:

- **Attribute directive**: This changes the appearance or behavior of an element. One example for this can be the NgStyle directive from Angular core.
- **Structural directive**: This manipulates the DOM, just like NgFor and NgSwitch from the Angular core.

Directives as opposed to components, do not require a template, and usually define a selector as an attribute.

Preparing our development environment

Like for previous chapters, let's create a new project as explained in *Chapter 2, Setting Up an Angular 2 Development Environment with angular-cli*. You can also remove all the existing folders and remove all the unnecessary code from `app.component.ts`:

```
[app.component.ts]
import { Component } from '@angular/core';

@Component({
  selector: 'app-root',
  template: `<h1>Angular2 components</h1>`
})
export class AppComponent {}
```

The basic attribute directive

Let's begin by creating a new file for our directive named `text-marker.ts`. Inside it, paste the following code:

```
[text-marker.ts]
import { Directive, ElementRef, Renderer } from '@angular/core';

@Directive({
  selector: '[text-marker]'
})
export class TextMarker {
  constructor(element: ElementRef, renderer: Renderer) {
    renderer.setElementStyle(element.nativeElement,
      'text-decoration', 'underline');
  }
}
```

To create a directive, we need to import the `Directive` decorator function from Angular core. We will also need two more classes named `ElementRef` and `Renderer` to manipulate the element. They are injected to our directive class from its constructor.

This directive will add styling to the element and decorate the text with an underline.

Let's test this directive by applying it on our `app component` template. Open `index.ts` and add the following code:

```
[app.component.ts]
import { Component } from '@angular/core';

@Component({
  selector: 'app-root',
  template: `<h1 text-marker>Angular2 components</h1>`
})
export class AppComponent {}
```

Don't forget to add the `TextMarker` class to the `declarations` attribute of the root module. This operation will be required for all custom components and directives implemented in this chapter. Open the `app.module.ts` file and update it as described here:

```
[app.module.ts]
import { BrowserModule } from '@angular/platform-browser';
import { NgModule } from '@angular/core';
import { FormsModule } from '@angular/forms';
import { HttpModule } from '@angular/http';
import { AppComponent } from './app.component';
import { TextMarker } from './text-marker';

@NgModule({
  declarations: [
    AppComponent,
    TextMarker
  ],
  imports: [
    BrowserModule,
    FormsModule,
    HttpModule
  ],
  providers: [],
  bootstrap: [AppComponent]
})
export class AppModule { }
```

Open the browser and inspect the result:

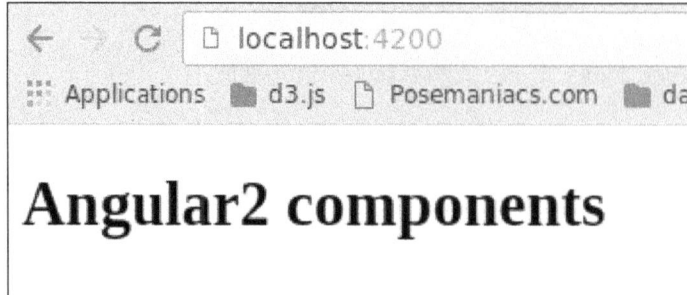

ElementRef and Renderer

Attribute directives intend to add behavior to an element. For this, we need to gain access to the element itself. In Angular 2, direct access to a DOM element is considered to be bad practice. Angular keeps the code separated from the view layer by introducing an abstraction layer.

To reference the element, we use ElementRef, which is the class that represents the type of element of the platform we are running on. In our case, it's the browser DOM. The ElementRef class has the ability to reveal the native element that it wraps, but we won't need it. Instead, we will use another class named Renderer and pass the ElementRef instance to it. Renderer is a class that exposes methods for manipulating the element, without specifying which type of element it is. This mechanism keeps our code decoupled from the element's implementation.

Reacting to events from the host element

An attribute directive applies on an element. If we want to react to the events that this element fires, we can use the HostListener decorator on some methods of the Directive class. In the following example, our directive will listen to mouse events from the element and change the style in response:

```
[text-marker.ts]
import {
Directive, ElementRef, Renderer, HostListener
} from '@angular/core';

@Directive({
 selector: '[text-marker]'
})
export class TextMarker {
```

```
constructor(private element: ElementRef,
private renderer: Renderer) { }

@HostListener('mouseenter')
markText() {
  this.renderer.setElementStyle(
    this.element.nativeElement,
    'text-decoration',
    'underline'
  );
}

@HostListener('mouseleave')
unmarkText() {
  this.renderer.setElementStyle(
    this.element.nativeElement,
    'text-decoration',
    ''
  );
}
}
```

Now, the style will be applied and removed each time the mouse enters and leaves the element that *host* the attribute directive.

Passing properties to the directive

We can also pass configuration into the directive by using properties. Just like components, directives can declare inputs. Let's refactor our `Directive` class to fetch and apply a text color from a property

```
[text-marker.ts]
import {
  Directive,
  ElementRef,
  Renderer, Input,
  HostListener
} from '@angular/core';

@Directive({
  selector: '[text-marker]'
})
export class TextMarker {
  @Input('text-marker')
  private color: string;

  constructor(
```

```
      private element: ElementRef,
      private renderer: Renderer
  ){ }

  @HostListener('mouseenter')
  onEnter() {
    this.applyStyle(this.color, true);
  }
  @HostListener('mouseleave')
  onExit() {
    this.applyStyle('', false);
  }

  private applyStyle(
    color:string, mark:boolean) {

      // apply underline
      this.renderer.setElementStyle(
        this.element.nativeElement,
        'text-decoration',
        mark ? 'underline' : ''
      );

      // apply color
      this.renderer.setElementStyle(
        this.element.nativeElement
        'color', color
      );
    }
}
```

By using the `Input` decorator, we can accept the value of the property (in our case, it is `text-marker`) and use it inside our directive class. Now we can pass the color that we want to use. Open `app.component.ts` and try the following code:

```
[app.component.ts]
import { Component } from '@angular/core';

@Component({
  selector: 'app-root',
  template: `<h1 text-marker="red">Angular2 components</h1>`
})
export class AppComponent {}
```

Now, each time the mouse enters the h1 element, the text should be colored in red and decorated with an underline:

The basic structural directive

As we mentioned at the beginning of this chapter, the third type of directive is called structural directives, and as the name suggests, those directives are meant to manipulate the element that they applied on. Angular core includes several directives that manipulate the DOM, such as ngIf, ngFor, and ngSwitch.

For our example, we will implement our own ngIf directive that behaves just like the original one.

First, create a new file named only-if.ts and let's define the basic structure for our directive:

```
[only-if.ts]
import { Directive } from '@angular/core';

@Directive({
  selector: '[onlyIf]'
})
export class OnlyIf {
}
```

The structural directives begin their lives just like an attribute directive. We import the @Directive decorator from the Angular core and declare the selector as an attribute.

Next, we will need to access the template, and we will need some kinds of container so we can attach or remove views. For this, we will need to inject `TemplateRef` and `ViewContainerRef`:

```
[only-if.ts]
import {
  Directive,
  TemplateRef,
  ViewContainerRef
} from '@angular/core';

@Directive({
  selector: '[onlyIf]'
})
export class OnlyIf {
  constructor(private _templateRef: TemplateRef,
              private _viewContainerRef: ViewContainerRef)
  {  }
}
```

Our directive, just like the Angular `ngIf`, needs to receive a Boolean from its caller that represents the condition on which the content will be shown or removed. For this, we will declare an input for this condition and make use of `ViewContainerRef` and `TemplateRef`:

```
[only-if.ts]
import {
  Directive,
  Input,
  TemplateRef,
  ViewContainerRef
} from 'angular/core';

@Directive({
  selector: '[onlyIf]'
})
export class OnlyIf {
  constructor(private _templateRef: TemplateRef<any>,
              private _viewContainerRef: ViewContainerRef) {  }

  @Input()
  set onlyIf(condition:boolean) {
    if (condition) {
      this._viewContainerRef.createEmbeddedView(this._templateRef);
    } else {
      this._viewContainerRef.clear();
    }
  }
}
```

Let's make use of this directive. Open `app.component.ts` and paste the
following code:

```
[app.component.ts]
import { Component } from '@angular/core';

@Component({
  selector: 'app-root',
  template: `
    <input type="checkbox" [(ngModel)]="condition">
    <p *onlyIf="condition">
      This content will shown only if the condition is true
    </p>
  `
})
export class AppComponent {}
```

Don't forget to add the `OnlyIf` class to the `declarations` attribute of the
root module.

Let's explore what's going on: when we use the asterisk (*) to call our directive,
Angular creates a `<template>` tag behind the scenes. Inside our directive, we can
get a reference for this template through the `TemplateRef` class. Then, we can use
the `ViewContainerRef` class, which represents a `container` so that we can embed a
view into it, to create or clear a view from the content of the template.

Summary

In Angular 2, there are three types of directive: component directive, attribute
directive, and structural directive. Throughout this chapter, we got a quick
introduction to them and learned how to build simple directives. Directives
can do much more, but that's beyond the scope of this book.

Index

Symbols

.ts
  reference 22

A

accordion component
  about 67-76
  accordion tab, implementing 67
  life cycle 77-79
  tree, extending 76, 77
Ahead of Time (AoT) 30
Angular 1
  Model-View-Controller pattern 3
Angular 2
  about 15
  application, breaking into components 5, 6
  attribute directive 95
  components 95, 96
  development environment,
      preparing 65, 66, 85, 96
  directives 95, 96
  generating 9, 11, 12
  structural directive 95
Angular application
  bootstrapping 29, 30
angular-cli
  installing 9
  URL 9
annotations
  versus decorators 23
Application component 6
asterisk (*)
  about 49
  example 49

attribute directive
  about 95-97
  ElementRef class 98
  events, reacting from host element 98, 99
  properties, passing 99, 100
  Renderer class 98

B

basic types, TypeScript 20, 21
bootstrap
  collapse component 89-92
  dependencies, importing 85-87
  tooltip component 87-89
Button component 6

C

classes, in TypeScript 18, 19
collapse component
  reference link 89
components
  defining 4
component selector
  about 31, 32
  options 32, 33
component template
  about 33, 34
  styles, embedding in 35, 36
controller 2
core directives
  about 47
  NgClass directive 50, 51
  NgFor directive 53
  NgIf directive 48
  NgStyle directive 51, 52

NgSwitch directive 53
custom events
  emitting 59, 60
  local variable, referencing with 61, 63
custom types, TypeScript 21, 22

D

data
  passing, via properties 57-59
data bindings 41
data interpolation 43-47
decorators
  about 23
  using 22
  versus annotations 23
default exports 18
dependencies
  managing, with modules 17

E

ElementRef class 98
encapsulation mode
  about 40
  emulated 40
  example 40
  native 40
  none 40
event binding 55
events
  reacting, from host element 98
export statement 17

F

Form component 6

G

generics
  about 22
  reference 22

H

host element
  events, reacting from 98, 99

I

import statement 17
inline template
  example 34
Input component 6
integrated development environment (IDE)
  selecting 13

L

life cycle events
  about 83
  interfaces 79
  OnChanges method 81, 83
  OnDestroy method 79, 80, 81
  OnInit method 79, 80, 81
local variable
  example 61
  referencing with 61, 63
Long Time Support(LTS)
  URL 8

M

model 2
Model-View-Controller pattern
  controller 2
  in Angular 1 3
  model 2
  view 2
  working 1, 2
Model View ViewModel (MVVM)
  about 3
  model 3
  view 3
  ViewModel 3
modules
  about 17
  default exports 18
  dependencies, managing with 17
  export statement 17
  import statement 17

N

NgClass directive 50, 51
NgFor directive
  about 53
  example 53
NgIf directive
  about 48
  asterisk (*) 49
NgStyle directive
  about 51, 52
  example 51
NgSwitch directive 53
node
  about 7
  installing 8
  URL 8
npm
  about 7
  installing 8
  URL 8

O

OnChanges method 81, 83
OnDestroy method 79-81
OnInit method 79-81

P

properties
  data, passing via 57-59
property binding 54

Q

Query children components
  example 63
  parent component, used 63

R

Renderer class 98

S

shadow DOM 36-40
structural directive
  about 95, 101, 103
  example 101
styles 35
styles property 35

T

TaskList component 6
TaskRow component 6
  checkbox 6
  label 6
  trash 6
template strings 34
two-way data binding 55
TypeScript 15, 16
TypeScript interfaces
  URL 79
type system
  about 20
  basic types 20, 21
  custom types 21, 22
  generics 22
typings
  URL 22

V

view
  about 2
  switching, to components 4
ViewModel 3
VSCode
  URL 13

W

webstorm
  reference link 13

www.ingramcontent.com/pod-product-compliance
Lightning Source LLC
Chambersburg PA
CBHW082104210326
41599CB00033B/6576